Advanced Praise

Memoirs ultimately come down to two things—the teller and the tale. In Joanne Flynn Black's *In Motion*, the tale is marvelous, a trip around the world where the usual adventures are interrupted by everything from conveying marriage proposals across international lines to giant beetle attacks ("cell phones with legs"). But what really sticks with you is the teller. Joanne achieved her career dream only to find it wasn't such a dream after all. When she risks it all to pursue another life—travel, adventure, love, family, *and* career—she is revealed to be the same hapless, utterly lost person we all are, but always with a shrug and a smile that makes you love her all the more. A delightful book.

John Yearley, award-winning playwright,
TV writer, and teacher

Joanne's witty way with words will instantly transport you straight to the scene of her engaging travel stories. I shared her laughter, her anxiety, and the roller coaster ride of emotions as she navigated her round-the-world trip. Enjoy the ride...and beware of desert beetles!

Beth Santos, author of *Wander Woman: How to Reclaim Your Space, Find Your Voice, and Travel the World, Solo*

Joanne Flynn Black's oh-so-readable globe-spinning tales of adventure, love, lust, and wanderlust prove that sometimes the worst trips make the best stories. *In Motion* is a compendium of travel tales illuminating how we humans live by universal truths, no matter where we're born, but also our differences from each other, which make travel the most interesting activity we can do. The second-best activity would be reading about it in Joanne Flynn Black's wonderful book.

David Farley, author of *An Irreverent Curiosity: In Search of the Church's Strangest Relic in Italy's Oddest Town*

Exhilarating! *In Motion* had me laughing, crying, and experiencing all the emotions on this rollercoaster of life and worldwide adventures. Throw in a love story with Ira and amazing characters from around the world—this is a journey that we all need to take. Intrepid travelers who prove time and time again that the best adventures are found in the moments with strangers and friends. Joanne's storytelling is filled with openness, curiosity, courage, and a willingness to say "YES" to the biggest adventure of all: falling in love.

Nora Ring, avid solo traveler and founder of Solotravelz

In Motion by Joanne Flynn Black is a captivating journey of self-discovery, adventure, and love. Joanne takes us on a thrilling adventure that spans fourteen countries and 31,000 miles. This book is all about embracing the unknown—both in travel and in matters of the heart. With wit, elegance, and a warm, inviting spirit, Joanne navigates the unpredictable twists of her journey and romance, offering readers an inspiring tale of courage, exploration, and transformation. *In Motion* is a must-read for anyone who dreams of taking charge of their life and chasing after the adventures that call to their soul.

Jill Celeste, MA, author of *Loud Woman: Goodbye, Inner Good Girl!*

Joanne Flynn Black lives a dream many of us only fantasize about, and, as the chapters unfold swiftly, the reader is swept along—true to the title *In Motion*—on Flynn Black's exhilarating journey. Confronted with pivotal questions: Will her pursuit of independence outweigh love? Can one chase lifelong personal adventure alongside a partner? The narrative keeps you guessing about the thrills of travel and the complexities of love. At its core, it delves into the essence of humanity.

Lisa Tognola, author of *As Long As It's Perfect*

Joanne Flynn Black's *In Motion* is an adventurous and heart-warming story that pulls you right in. When Joanne steps away from her corporate career to see the world, she ends up on a wild ride across fourteen countries and 31,000 miles. From camel rides in India to dodging bulls in Spain, her journey is full of surprises—including a just as unpredictable romance. Told with humor and honesty, *In Motion* is a fun reminder that life's best adventures often happen when you take a leap of faith.

Stephanie Fritts, CEO of Exec Wranglers and coauthor
of *Heart-Centered Marketing*

IN MOTION

IN MOTION

Around the World in Love and Heartbreak

JOANNE FLYNN BLACK

Foreword by
DON GEORGE

Edited by
DEBORAH KEVIN

HIGHLANDER
PRESS

Paperback ISBN: 978-1-956442-40-3
Ebook ISBN: 978-1-956442-99-1
Library of Congress Control Number: Applied For.

Published by Highlander Press
A division of Highlander Enterprises, LLC
501 W. University Pkwy, Ste. B2
Baltimore, MD 21210

Cover design: Hanne Broter (https://yourbrandvision.com/)
Cover photographs: Ira L. Black (https://www.iralblack.com/) and Joanne Flynn Black
Author photo: Ira L. Black (https://www.iralblack.com/)

To Al Black for always encouraging me to write this book,
even when I wanted to "shelve" the project;

To our parents—Madeline, Joe, Helen, and Al—who followed us (via long-
distance phone calls) each step of the way;

To my son, Joe Black, who makes our family adventures even more fun with his
view of the world; and

To Ira Black for taking his chances and joining me on this journey of life.

Contents

Foreword

LESSONS ON LIFE'S UNPREDICTABLE PATH

Don George

In Motion presents an immediately intriguing premise: Joanne Flynn Black, a rising star in an iconic consulting company, decides to press pause on her corporate ascent to let go of her stress, expand her horizons, and have some adventures in the wide world.

Then an attractive stranger enters the scene. Romance waxes as the days until departure wane. Should she still pursue her dream of a solo around-the-world fling? Or flip her plan upside-down and take on a traveling companion who may end up being a life companion?

The choice is made and the couple take off together.

The geographical and emotional odyssey that ensues covers 31,000 miles in fourteen countries. The two survive a car breakdown in New Zealand, a desert beetle-plagued camel safari in India, and a water-soaked Songkran festival in Thailand. They find themselves dead-ending in the dark on a campervan tour of Tasmania, praying to a fertility god in a back-alley temple in Bhutan, meeting a trailblazing woman spice-seller in Jodhpur, delivering a love letter from a smitten Indian tour guide to a former client in Moscow, exploring off-the-beaten-path attractions with a gregarious coffee-roaster in Lithuania, befriending a stranger who offers them a behind-the-scenes tour of the

Kremlin, and narrowly avoiding a charging bull at the running of the bulls in Spain.

As they share these marvels and misadventures, the route of their romance proves as unpredictable as the route of their journey, and the scenario that had been playing in Black's mind again gets flipped upside-down. Where will this trip lead? How do we find—and stay on—the path that will take us to our dreams?

In Motion recounts this zigzagging journey with a beguiling mixture of innocence, honesty, humor, grace, wonder, and wisdom. Black is a passionate adventuress who embraces the places and peoples she encounters with a winningly wide open heart and mind. As she does so, her tale artfully interweaves four timely themes: taking charge of our life, envisioning and actually doing the trip we seek, welcoming worldly differences in culture and cuisine, and navigating the twists and turns of love's ever-changing scene.

In the end, Black presents a moving parable of encounter and lesson, both global and personal, that is expansive, insightful, and joyously life-transforming; her odyssey "around the world in love and heartbreak" ultimately illuminates the path we all should take.

Twenty-Two People in a Boat

I'M IN A BOAT WITH TWENTY-ONE OTHERS. WE'RE PADDLING for our lives. Someone is shouting commands at us, "

Longer!

Deeper!

Harder!"

Chaos is all around us.

We're looking straight ahead.

We need to get there quickly.

Water is getting in the boat.

And then we see it! The finish line. We're in a Dragon Boat race in Lake Merced, San Francisco.

My team, the AquaAssassins, is in the lead.

I don't have time to think about the history of Dragon Boating, which originated in China more than 2000 years ago. I only know that I want us to win. All twenty paddlers, one drummer, and one steersperson have one thing on our mind: Crossing the finish line first.

And to do that we have to be paddling in exact unison. All twenty paddles need to enter and exit the water at the same moment. To gain momentum. To lift the boat from the water and glide. That is why the drummer yelling out commands plays such an important role on this narrow, forty-foot-long boat.

And equally important as the drummer are the paddlers being part of a team. Teamwork. Togetherness.

As we cross the finish line and see that we made it there first, there is whooping and high-fives. I feel a certain love for my team-mates. We're like a family. We practiced three times per week together to get to this point. And after each practice we spend time together at someone's house or a restaurant.

After our celebration, I say goodbye with what feels like hundreds of hugs. I'm driving my steel-gray two-seater BMW M Roadster convertible down a steep road in the Presidio Heights, San Francisco. It feels good to grip the leather of the steering wheel and the stick shift handle. The steep hills scare some stick-shift drivers, but not me. I'm a master of the hills in this car.

The top is down, of course. The music is blasting "You Oughta Know" by Alanis Morrisette, and I'm singing along.

I've got my wooden dragon boat paddle balanced vertically between the two seats, sticking up like a shark's fin for the world to see.

What could be cooler?

My thoughts drift to how I have all of this in my life. How did I get to be so lucky? My job, the foundation on which my amazing life is built.

It's not lost on me how far I've come. Born and raised on the other side of the country, in Jersey City, New Jersey. I didn't attend a big-name university, yet I've landed at one of the most prestigious and most competitive consulting organizations. Deloitte Consulting. Considered one of the "Big 6" firms.

I've climbed up the corporate ladder and now I'm almost at the top. Senior Manager. Next rung up is Partner. Deloitte has an "up or out" policy. Keep moving up or get pushed off the ladder.

I think about all of the late nights I had this week - deadlines and priorities and revisions. I realize I'm working hard with long hours, while keeping an SEE (Substantially Exceeds Expectations) rating. But that is what life is about.

Isn't it?

I'm snapped back into reality when the radio starts playing one of my favorite songs, Alanis Morrisette's "Isn't It Ironic?"

I'm singing along.

I turn to the passenger seat to sing along with someone.

But no one is there. No one to share this fantastic life with.

Just my PFD—my personal flotation device—for the boat.

Him, Window. Me, Aisle. Red Eye Flight

NOVEMBER 1995

I'M HEADING TO NEW JERSEY FOR MY NEPHEW DYLAN'S christening, my first experience at being a godmother. I decide to take the overnight flight, the red eye, to maximize my time. Why not just sleep on the plane and get there ready to seize the day?

I have lots of practice sleeping on planes, since my job requires me to be onsite Monday morning in whatever city I'm working in. I never want to lose my Sunday to flying all day, so I take the overnight flight.

I get my sleep and when I arrive early Monday morning, heading right to my client. Well, after a trip to the ladies' room to change from my sweatpants to my business suit.

So, tonight is no different. I'm ready with my eye shades, neck pillow, and Bose noise cancellation headphones. I slip into my seat and I'm all ready to tune the world out and get some rest. And then I see my row mate. He's at the window. I'm in the aisle seat. With no one in the middle seat.

"Hi, I'm Ira," he says, and I introduce myself.

"What's taking you to New Jersey?" he asks.

"My nephew's christening," I say. "I'm the godmother."

And my eyeshades do not go on.

We talk.

And my noise cancellation headphones stay in their case.

And we talk some more.

He's witty and smart and has a way with words.

We talk for six hours straight. When we get to New Jersey, he walks me to the baggage claim. And then to my rental car. We say goodbye and exchange business cards.

"Maybe we could meet for coffee while you're here?" he asks.

I never call while I'm in New Jersey. My trip is full of family and friends and the fear that "coffee" might turn into more than coffee. I'm dating someone back in San Francisco. It doesn't feel right to make that call.

However, we have each other's numbers, and maybe one day we will see each other.

Calling from SFO

RING.

Ring.

Ring.

My roommate yells, "I think it's for you," when she sees the 917 number displayed on the caller ID on our shared phone.

"Hello." I answer hesitantly because I also don't know that area code.

"Hey, Joanne. It's Ira, I'm calling you from the San Francisco airport." For the eight years since we met, we've kept in touch occasionally over email, and, less frequently, the occasional phone call. Either I had a boyfriend or he had a girlfriend. It seemed that we were never single at the same time. I was thinking, "wow, he's in San Francisco. And calling."

"Hey, Ira. Great to hear from you. How long will you be in town?" I ask.

"Oh, well, I'm in the airport and heading home to New Jersey."

"I'm sorry, you're calling to let me know you're here but heading home?"

"Umm, yeah," he replies.

"I have to say that it's kind of ridiculous that you're calling me from the airport when you are leaving. Why didn't you call me when you were here?"

Dead silence on the other end of the line, punctuated by the background noise of the airport.

"Here's the deal. How about the next time we are on each other's coast we make an agreement to call each other?" I say.

"Yes, let's do that. It's a deal," Ira says.

So, we have a deal.

We've made a pact.

Lady Liberty

FEBRUARY 2003

I ARRIVE IN NEW YORK FOR WORK, CLOSE TO DELOITTE'S World Financial Center location. I'm staying at a hotel overlooking the Statue of Liberty. My trip will last for three weeks, which is plenty of time to finally meet Ira for that coffee we talked about eight years ago.

Ring.

Ring.

He answers.

"Hey, Ira, guess what? I'm in New York," I say.

"Guess what? I'm in San Francisco," he replies.

"Oh no way. Did we literally just pass each other in the air?" I giggle. How ironic.

"No, I've been here for a month," he replies.

I stop laughing.

"But I thought we had an agreement?" I say, realizing he didn't keep his word.

Dead silence on the other end of the line as I realize that I'm the only one of us who kept their word on this deal. I'm feeling perplexed. And outraged.

The Beauty Bar

IT'S FRIDAY NIGHT. I FINISH UP MY EAST COAST WORK TRIP and head back to my home in San Francisco. Ira is still on his work project there.

Ring.

Ring.

Ring.

"Hey sorry about not holding up my end of the deal. Can we meet now that we're both in the same place?" Ira asks.

"Sure, we can meet," I say, in an annoyed tone. I'm going to meet him, but it's mostly because I plan to tell him off. Who the hell does this guy think he is? I'm thinking that it will be poetic justice to meet him and make it obvious what he has just missed.

Ira calls the night that we plan to meet to find out the logistics for our first in-person connection in over eight years. "Where would you like to meet?" he asks. I can hear in his tone that he's unaware that I'm coming to meet him just to tell him off.

"I'll pick you up and we can head together to the Mission district," I say. I purposely take a little extra time to make sure I'm looking as smoking as my roadster. It's a cool San Francisco evening, but impressions need to be made and a boy needs to be taught a lesson on how to be a man. I pull up around the circular driveway of his downtown hotel, my car top down and music blaring a No Doubt song. Ira is standing outside waiting for me. He is wearing a jean jacket with a colored shirt. He doesn't seem to know what's about to hit him.

I'm wearing my furry jacket which is a combination of sexy and rugged all rolled into one and my favorite lip gloss for added "killa factor."

"Hop in," I say.

He opens the door, slides in, and I pull away.

"It's been a long time," he says.

"Yes, it has," I say, shifting the gears extra forcefully. In my head I'm saying, "One of us held up their end of the bargain."

Where are you taking me?" he asks, with an air of hesitation about being a prisoner in my car.

"To the Mission. There's a cool bar there," I say.

After navigating the streets of San Francisco, we arrive at our destination, The Beauty Bar. A dive-ish bar that is set up like a beauty parlor from the 1950s, complete with a nail polish station and a drink named Prell. They even have old school hair dryers that lines of women would sit under. It gives the place an incredibly cool, underground feeling. I can tell by Ira's reaction that he's digging the vibe.

We sit at the bar and order two Prells.

It's early for the bar scene, so we have the whole place to ourselves.

We talk and drink and talk some more. He's as charming and funny as the day we met on the plane. And then I remember why I'm here.

"So why didn't you keep up your end of the pact?" I ask. I'm so ready to tell him off. I have practiced the speech in my full-length mirror.

"Well, I had a girlfriend, and I wasn't sure if after all this time coffee really meant coffee or something else," he says.

"Oh," I say. I'm a little shocked. This isn't the response I had rehearsed in my mirror. I guess I can't be mad at him for honoring his relationship. I'm dating someone at the time as well. We're on again and off again, but at this moment we're technically on.

Ira apologizes for not calling me and says that he's glad that I came to meet him. He tells me that he is worried that I was only coming to tell him off because I sounded so angry on the phone.

My anger diminishes the more we talk. I kinda like this guy.

And then he says, "It seems like you're working pretty hard at Deloitte." He starts massaging my shoulders. In the bar. Again, who the hell does this guy think he is? Except that I'm enjoying it and I can really use the stress relief.

We finish our drinks and I ask if he wants to get something to eat.

The Luna Cafe across the street is where we become two people trying to get to know each other, not one person trying to settle a score and another trying to save his own life.

I feel the same connection I felt on the plane. He tells me he feels it too. Although this time it's on the ground. We enjoy our time at dinner and then leave. Time flies by.

As I'm dropping him back at his hotel, he says, "I'm here another day. Want to meet for dinner tomorrow?"

I'm conflicted because meeting up with a guy from my life eight years ago seemed like an okay thing to do even though I'm dating someone else. But meeting a second time is clearly crossing a boundary.

Still, I find myself saying, "Yes," while wondering what I'm doing.

The next night we go to a Moroccan restaurant and sit on pillows on the floor, enjoying our time together.

As I chow down on my chicken tagine, there's a commentary running on a loop in my head, *"Are we friends? Is this turning into something else? Where is this leading?"*

On Sunday, Deloitte is having a celebration event at a fancy restaurant in downtown San Francisco. I'm chatting with my coworker and friend, Allison, telling her all about my weekend activities with my new/old friend Ira.

"When is he leaving?" Allison asks.

"Tonight, on a red eye."

"That's ironic. You're taking a red eye to your client in Kansas City tonight. Maybe you'll run into each other at the airport."

"Maybe. He did keep asking me which flight I'm going to be on," I say. "But I think I'm going to switch mine to an earlier flight, since this party seems like it's letting up."

And then it hits me. Did Ira ask me about my flight because he was thinking of switching to the same flight? It did have a layover in Chicago. And the flight path from Chicago to New Jersey is a standard route.

I realize my head must be swelling from all his attention. Why would anyone switch from a direct to a connecting flight just so they could be on the same plane as me?

I'm about to call the Deloitte travel line to ask them to switch mine to an earlier flight when something stops me. I decide to make a different call. "Hey Ira. It's me. I have an odd question for you."

"Hey. Good to hear from you. What's up?"

"Remember I said I am taking the red eye flight to Chicago and then Kansas City tonight?"

"Yeah, I do."

"Well, I'm thinking of changing it to an earlier one. This Deloitte dinner is going to wrap up soon and then I won't have to wait around. You wouldn't have happened to switch your direct flight to be on this one with me, would you?"

There's silence on the other end of the line. It continues. More silence. And then, "You'll have to keep your original flight to find out," he says.

What kind of answer is that? Who the hell does this guy think he is? This is becoming a recurring question.

I decide to stay at the event longer and keep my original flight. The drinks are flowing. The more I think about this, the more I say to myself, "He better be there."

I hop into a cab for the airport. I know the drill. I've flown out of this airport mostly every week of my eight years at Deloitte.

I arrive at the gate. I look around.

No Ira.

I walk around in case I've missed him. No Ira.

I start pacing back and forth. Is this some kind of cruel joke? I could've been halfway to my destination already if I'd switched my flight. Just then I see a familiar jean jacket—with Ira wearing it.

I'm shocked but not shocked. And I'm glad I didn't change my flight!

"I'm glad my hunch was right!"

I said, laughing, "But your original one had no stops. This has a layover." As an experienced traveler, I realize what a big sacrifice this is. I also realize that I'm slurring my words a little bit, and that I drank way more at the Deloitte party than I should have.

"I think they called our boarding section," he says.

"I wonder if we're sitting near each other?" I ask.

"Yes, I'm right next to you."

"How'd you manage that?"

"I have my ways."

We board the plane, and he is right. He is sitting next to me. I imagine him sweet talking the ticket agent to get a seat next to me.

"Well, this is going to be like old times," I say, remembering our hours of talking all night on that first flight together.

I imagine all the people around are slightly annoyed because we're talking, and they are trying to sleep.

"Items may have shifted in flight. Please be careful when opening the overhead bins," the flight attendant says.

Wait. *What?*

I turn to Ira with a confused look. "We just got settled in. What's this announcement about landing?"

"Yeah, we're here. We're landing in Chicago," Ira says.

I still look confused.

"You fell asleep and were out the whole flight," he says.

"No," I say, my response coming out as a wail. I feel so bad that Ira switched his flight to be with me and all I did was fall asleep on him. Literally, sleeping with my head on his shoulder.

We leave the plane and walk toward our gates for our final destinations: Kansas City, Kansas for me; and Newark, New Jersey for him.

He gets me settled at my gate. It's five in the morning. My next flight isn't for two hours, so I make a little nest to get a little more sleep. I know I have to be on my game and appear well rested at the client site.

"Do you have any kind of alarm? What if you fall asleep and miss your flight?" Ira asks.

"I'll be fine. I imagine I'll hear the boarding call."

"But what if you don't? What if you sleep through it?"

I am fairly certain I won't miss the connecting flight, but this night has already had so many unexpected things happen, I'm not sure.

"Here, take my watch. I'll set an alarm for you."

"I can't take your watch. You'll be without one."

"I have another one at home," Ira says. "Here, take it."

Ira slips the watch off his wrist and puts it on mine.

"But how will I get it back to you?" I ask.

"We'll figure it out," he says.

And just like that he has to leave to catch his flight.

I think about the kindness that he showed me. I'm not used to being taken care of like this. Who is this guy, anyway?

Birthday in Santa Barbara

MAY 2003

RING.

Ring.

Ring.

"Hey Joanne, my work is taking me to Santa Barbara in a few weeks," Ira says. "I was wondering if you'd want to meet me there?"

Silence.

"I know it's not super close to San Francisco, but it's at least in the same state, so I figured I'd ask."

"When is it?" I ask.

"It's the weekend of May 30th."

"Hmmm. Well, my birthday is on the thirty-first, so it's my birthday weekend. I'm not sure what I'm up to."

The truth is, I know I need to leave Tyler. There's no way I'm hopping on a plane to meet Ira with another guy still in my life. I wonder why I'm still hanging around with Tyler anyway. We're clearly not meant to be.

Earlier this year, I spent a few months working in London. Tyler had a work gig in London too. I got to take him to fancy dinners on my expense account, which helped fund his trip. When it was time for me to head home, he took me to the airport—and broke up with me. I spent the whole flight perplexed about what had happened. I'm not really sure how we wound up back together.

"Well," I say to Ira, "there is something I need to take care of before I can answer that."

Two days later, I get a call from Ira.

"Hey, have you thought any more about Santa Barbara?"

Are you kidding me? It's all I've thought about for the last twenty-four hours. "Here's the deal. I'm thinking about it. But I need do something first," I say. I'm not sure if he understands what my vagueness is about. I decide to tell him. "You know I'm in a relationship with someone. I need to end that before seeing you again."

Ira decides to up the stakes by making my stay the equivalent of Club Med. "There's nothing you need to plan or worry about. Nothing. Just show up." He even calls it "Club Ira."

When the plane touches down in Santa Barbara, I see Ira holding a "Club Ira" homemade sign.

I laugh.

We have the most amazing time together.

And never look back.

We start dating even though we live on different coasts.

East Coast/West Coast

JUNE 2003

THE BLESSING IN DISGUISE IS THAT WE BOTH HAVE corporate jobs for which we need to travel weekly from Monday to Thursday.

The weekends are ours and we are free to fly on the company's nickel wherever we want to be.

"I'm in Providence, Rhode Island, at the Westin in their heavenly bed," I say.

"I'm in Seattle at the Westin in their heavenly bed," Ira says.

"Do you want to fly to me?" one of us says. We spend lots of time at the beginning of our relationship crisscrossing the country. Every weekend.

Kansas. Rhode Island. California. New Jersey. New Mexico.

Wherever.

It's always an adventure.

"When are we going to meet this guy?" my friend Allison asks.

"In a few weeks, we're going to be in San Francisco. I'm going to schedule a night out where he can meet all my friends," I say.

"And what if we don't approve?"

"You will. He's quite loveable."

"You see each other a lot," Allison says.

"Yeah, well, our jobs make it easy to do that," I say.

"Ira's on the three-day rule," Allison says.

"The three-day rule?" I ask.

"He needs to see you no more than three days apart."

I do the math. Since I typically see Ira from Thursday night to Monday morning, I see her point.

I think back to my conversation with my roommate this morning, "You see your boyfriend more than I see mine. And mine lives twenty miles away in Palo Alto!"

I laugh it off, but realize she also has a point.

OTB – On the Beach

SUMMER 2002

MY CLIENT PROJECT HAS JUST FINISHED, AND DELOITTE has found my next project, but that doesn't start for another month. Scheduling normally doesn't work this way. The less time in between projects, the better. But occasionally, a prolonged break occurs. When this happens at Deloitte, everyone calls it being "on the beach." OTB. This phrase suggests lying in the sun on the sand with fruity cocktails. Or Off-Track Betting. But in reality, it's not like either of these.

At Deloitte, OTB means, "You're in between two paying clients, so while you're not bringing in any billable revenue, we're going to let you help us write proposals and do other work to bring in more clients. Oh, and since we're paying you, we're going to work you to the bone."

Everyone in your work group is notified. So, you get lots of OTB work. Sometimes the hardest and longest I've worked has been when I'm OTB, often because there's a crazy deadline.

The silver lining of OTB is that you get lots of exposure with top partners, and it's always good to impress the partners because they can make or break you in your annual review. All it takes is a few comments of, "She was not really a team player while working on that proposal," and your "stock" goes down, sometimes a few notches and sometimes it plummets.

But at this point, I'm not interested in exposure. So, when I find out that I'm going to be OTB for a month, I decide that I will *really* be on the beach. In Thailand. I'm going to combine this beach trip with a dragon boat racing trip I have scheduled in Taipei. San Francisco and Taipei are "sister cities," so they've invited our team to compete.

I have lots of paid vacation stacked up and this trip is the perfect opportunity to use it. And I need the break. I've been working non-stop for eight years without taking any type of real break. A week or so here and there, but not much longer.

I approach the partner in charge and say that I'd like to use my vacation for this extended trip. I make sure to add that the reason I'm on this dragon boat racing team is because I was invited by a former client. I'm taking "team player" to the extreme.

The partner understands how doing sports-related competitions translates to having a go-get-'em attitude in business life. He himself rode his bike on the same mountains traveled on the Tour de France, and as part of his endurance training, routinely walked up and down the thirty-one flights of stairs in the emergency exit stairway with a backpack full of books. In a suit and tie.

Of course, he says "yes" and wishes me luck in the competition. And with a hint of sarcasm, he adds, "Don't bother coming back without the gold medal."

I laugh.

With that, I'm off work for a month. I fly to Taipei with my team and have an amazing time on and off the water. While we don't win the gold medal, we do win the bronze. I hope that will be good enough for the partner when I return to work.

After the competition, I fly to Thailand to relax and explore the islands, Koh Samui, Kao Pha Ngan, Kao Tao. Each is more beautiful than the one before. And more remote.

Life is blissful. I not only have no idea what time it is, the days blur together. Time doesn't really matter at all. I just need to know which day I'm departing. Other than that, I'm happy not knowing the days.

My world of never-ending meetings, client "deliverables," and earning an SEE rating on my annual review doesn't matter. All that matters is my next meal and which island I'm hopping off to.

When I check into a rented hut on the beach of Kao Pha Ngan, the woman at the front desk tells me the price: eight dollars a night. Or if I want, I can upgrade to a two-floor hut for only four dollars more a night. My life back home flashes before me. I've spent more than that at a Peet's coffee run for my office buddies.

The seed of an idea comes to me: I could travel here for a month for what I spend eating and drinking a couple of nights out in San Francisco. I could sell my mountain bike for another month. I could sell that armoire monolith, that's larger than life, for another month.

Everything in my life now equates to how long I could spend in Thailand.

Trip math.

Could I do this? Could I leave everything I've built in my life to take a break and travel? I decide that I want to put a pause on my job. And travel. I'm not sure how it will exactly work, but I'm committed to doing this.

Solo.

Girl out in the world.

Interruptions

I SIT DOWN AT THE CONFERENCE ROOM TABLE. I LOOK around. A few smiles but mostly serious business faces. I'm the only woman in the room. A normal occurrence in this world I'm in. After introductions, we get to business and the conversation is flying.

"What should we do about the acquisition and how will it impact the implementation timeline and our deliverables?"

I have an idea. I think it's a pretty good one. Or is it? I'm going to throw it out and see what people think. But I wait for the person who is talking to complete his thought. Interruptions are rude, I was taught by my mother. *Okay, this guy is about to finish talking and I'll mention the idea I'm thinking about. Is it good enough? Will they think it the dumbest thing they've heard?*

Then I'm snapped back to reality. The first guy was interrupted by the second, who continues talking. My idea is much better than his, but he's speaking loud and assertively.

Just then a third guy interrupts and says what he thinks is a good idea.

Wait! It's the same idea I had. But he spoke before I did and will get all the credit. I mentally beat myself up. *Why didn't I speak sooner?*

I have nothing to add. The conversation is all about what a great idea the last guy had. We exhaust this topic and break for coffee.

The partner sees me out in the hallway. "Hey Joanne. You should contribute more. It looks bad for you to just sit there with nothing to add to the conversation."

"But I had an idea and didn't want to int—"

"Hey James." The partner is interrupted. "Do you have a minute? I need to discuss something."

"Yeah sure," the partner replies. "Talk to you later, Joanne."

I stand there bewildered.

Do I even belong here? Do I need to be more aggressive?

Where are the women partners?

My Brother Robert: My Protector

1978

I'M ELEVEN YEARS OLD AND CROUCHED DOWN IN THE corner of the kitchen, back against the yellow-flowered wallpaper, trying to make myself smaller.

"Are you taking drugs again?" my mother yells at my brother Robert.

He is quiet.

She yells some more.

My father yells, too, which is not normal behavior for him. He's typically soft-spoken and funny. Truly, the best dad ever.

Robert talks but doesn't make much sense. Oh man, he is definitely on something.

"We've done everything for you. Put you in the best drug rehabs. What else can we do? You need to take control of your actions," my father says, his voice crackles with unshed tears.

My mother chimes in with a similar thought, but nothing is getting to my brother.

My parents are right. They have put him in the best rehab. I'm not sure how they can afford it.

Mackenzie Phillips was at the same rehab as my brother. I know she can afford it from the money she makes on *One Day at a Time*.

But my parents? Only my dad earns a paycheck while my mom raises me and my three brothers.

I know it's worth it. I want my brother to be better. He's always been my protector, my guardian. The one who looks out for me.

I'd overheard my brothers Ed and Mike talking about how Robert started taking drugs after his girlfriend left him. He loved her. How could she dump him?

Now everyone in the kitchen is yelling.

Tears stream down my face. I wipe them away with the back of my hand.

"Look what you are doing to your sister!" my mom screams.

Robert comes over to me and sits in the same position with me. I am still crying.

I manage to get out in between the tears. "Even if you don't stop for mommy and daddy. Or yourself. Would you at least stop for me?"

He hugs me. Now we are all crying.

"Yes. I'll do it for you. I swear. I'll try. It's. Just. So. Hard."

But he didn't.

He left us.

Left me.

~

THERE ARE LINES OUT THE DOOR TO MARSHELLO'S funeral home on Ege Avenue in Jersey City. Robert was loved by many. Short haired friends from his days as a gymnast. Long haired friends from his days as a musician.

Friends from his high school—Saint Peter's Prep. Days and days, it's all the same.

Tears and hugs and more tears. I hear phrases like, "He was so young. He was so talented. He had so much ahead of him. His poor mom and dad. His poor brothers. His poor little sister."

~

IT'S ALL A BLUR. TIME IS PASSING. I'M WAITING FOR ROBERT to get up. To say it's all a joke.

To say he would never leave me. And protect me always.

I don't go back to school for a week. It's super sad at home. We're all walking around in a haze. Especially my mom. I can't imagine what it's like to lose a child. It's not the right death order.

She's not herself, of course. None of us are. Will we ever be?

Park Fast

1991

"So I see here that you graduated with a Bachelor of Science in computer science," the interviewer says.

"Yes I did," I reply. "With a minor in business," I add.

I feel confident in my degree. It was not an easy one to get. Lots of coding and analyzing. And very much a male-dominated field. But I liked pushing myself. And since I'm the first kid to go to college in my family, I wanted the degree to be in something impressive that would lead to a good job.

After a few standard questions about strength, weaknesses, and why I'm a good fit for the job, my interviewer, who is also named Joanne asks, "What is the Excel function where you split apart numbers and letters in one cell to make it go into multiple cells?"

"Oh, that is @parse," I say.

"Really, you know this?"

She seemed surprised.

"Yes, I do. I use it all the time," I say.

In order to help pay tuition, I got a job at my college helping out Dr. Shimson Kinory on forecasting models. I wasn't sure exactly what he was forecasting, but I learned how to use Excel like a ninja. And I used the @parse function all the time since we were always working with enormous data sets.

"Could you show me? Here on my spreadsheet?" Joanne asks.

"Uh, sure," I reply, even though I think this an unconventional way to conduct an interview. I work my Excel magic on her spreadsheet, and it works exactly as planned.

"Whoa. I didn't know how to do this," she said. "And to be honest, I just needed it done for this spreadsheet. Thanks for the help."

"Not a problem," I say with a confident smile.

Two days later, I get the call. I got the job.

"YOU WORK FOR A PARKING COMPANY? ARE YOU PARKING cars?" my date asks.

"I'm not parking cars," I say. "I work in the office as an operational analyst."

Although I think about my onboarding where I actually did park cars for a few days at the NYC Hippodrome location. They want all employees to spend a few days in the field, so we know what they are going through to do their jobs. But I didn't divulge that tidbit to my date.

Park Fast also owns Manhattan Mini Storage, so when my next date asks me where I work, I reply, "At Edison, it's a property management company with locations across the country."

Interviewing at Deloitte

MARCH 1995

"HI BILL, IS THIS ABOUT THE TEMP JOB?"

"Actually, no I have a better opportunity that just presented itself."

"Oh great. What's the job?"

"It's for a Senior Consultant at Deloitte."

"Oh. Wow. Do you think I'm qualified?" I ask.

"Yes I do. They are looking for someone who has implemented Software 2000."

"Oh, I've...." I hesitate.

"But what?"

"I mean, I don't know but don't they normally look for Harvard or Stanford graduates?"

"Yes, sometimes. But it's worth a shot. "Okay, let's try it!" I'm feeling confident. And then it hits me. People never get a job on their first interview. People normally interview for months before getting an opportunity like this. I have nothing to lose. I'll go and do my best. It will be good to have one interview under my belt.

"So you've implemented Software 2000?" asks Jean, a Deloitte senior manager.

"I have. And recently went to the Software 2000 conference in San Francisco."

"That's great. It's the skill we are currently looking for. We have a few upcoming clients who want to implement that system. I see your degree is in Computer Science. That is also a plus."

I stare at her in disbelief. She doesn't seem concerned that I graduated from Jersey City State College. As a joke, the students who went there gave it the nickname, "Harvard on the Boulevard." I can't believe I'm interviewing at a place that normally takes Harvard graduates. Throughout the day I interview with four other people including the group's director.

One good thing I'm realizing by being across the country they really didn't know much about my college. I tried to talk it up as having cutting edge technology, which I thought it did, but wasn't quite sure our cutting edge would be as sharp as the real Harvard.

What's Six More Months?

2003

I'M STANDING OUTSIDE THE MANAGING PARTNER'S OFFICE at Deloitte. I'm on time for our scheduled meeting. We exchange pleasantries and I dive right in. "Mark, I wanted to talk to you about that leave of absence I mentioned to you back in March."

"Remind me about what you want to do again."

I explain to him that I'm looking to take a six-month leave of absence as soon as my current project is over, which will be in two months.

"Well, I'm glad you're here. I support you in this. And you're doing an amazing job at your client."

"Thanks. I appreciate that," I say.

"So amazing that they want to extend you another six months."

"Another six months?"

"I mean, you can say no, but it will look good for your path to partner to stick it out for a little bit. What's another six months in the big picture?"

Another half a year. Another delay. Another thing to keep me away from where I need to be. "Yeah, I see," I say.

"You can think about it. Whatever you want to do is fine. You've had such a great trajectory here making senior manager in nine years.

I want to make sure you don't lose momentum by taking this little trip."

Little trip? Is he belittling me? This trip will be what keeps me sane. Working at Deloitte for nine years has taken a toll on my life.

Clients bring in Deloitte for a couple of reasons. Either they are making a big change in their organization, or they are implementing a big system which will take years to implement. The client goes through this upheaval, finishes the project, and goes back to work life as normal. For the consultants, we get to finish the project and then get thrown into another project.

I do love the newness though. The starting over. What I don't love is having to prove myself at each start of a new project. It's like the first day of school. Over and over again. And because they're paying us good money, they treat us like they own us.

I'M OUT FOR DRINKS WITH SOME FRIENDS AND I TELL THEM about my conversation with Mark.

"What are you going to do?" Eddy asks.

"I think I'm going to take the extension," I say.

"Why is that? Weren't you planning to take your trip when you were done with this client?"

"Yeah, I just don't want to piss everyone off at Deloitte by bailing on them."

"Why do you care?" he asks.

"Why do I care? Well, for one, they pay me lots of money. And for two, if I want to make partner when I come back, I need to leave on good terms."

Eddy shakes his head.

"OK, well, here's to more cosmos until you leave. Or should I say if you leave?"

Isaac Newton

2003

 "Objects at rest tend to stay at rest. Objects in motion tend to stay in motion."

Sir Isaac Newton

"OH YEAH, I'VE BEEN MEANING TO ASK YOU. WHAT'S UP with your signature line?"

"What do you mean?" My brain is a little fuzzy from lots of late nights at work topped off by multiple cosmos.

"Isaac Newton?" he says with a smirk. "Since when are *you* a physicist?"

I picture my email signature block that includes this quote, "Objects at rest tend to stay at rest. Objects in motion tend to stay in motion." I say, "Oh, that. Well, it reminds me that my lifestyle is keeping me in motion. And that's a good thing, right? I mean, who wants to stay at rest?"

He laughs. Did I notice a smirk?

"I'm going to do this trip. I just need to get some more things lined up," I say.

We go back to drinking our cosmos.

Meet the Parents: New Jersey

APRIL 2003

WE DECIDED TO SPEND THE WEEKEND IN NEW JERSEY. AND meet each other's parents. I meet Helen and Al Black. Ira meets Madeline and Joe Flynn.

Helen and Al remind me a little of George Costanza's parents from Seinfeld, but with more love. My dad is a kind, softspoken yet funny man. My mom is feisty.

My parents love that Ira is a Jersey boy, and hope that, because of him, I will come back to live in my home state. He is different from our family. Not Italian. Not Catholic. But they can see that he makes me happy and they are happy about that.

Ira's parents love that I'm originally from New Jersey and am part of Ira's life, yet they're concerned that I live all the way in California. And Helen doesn't really understand this trip I'm planning. "Doesn't she want to get married and start her life?" she tells Ira in private. Ira's parents are also worried that Ira will get this cockamamie idea and move to California.

We compare dinners with our families. With his, there's lot of cross talk around the table. People are yelling to be heard. People are yelling to yell. Lots of love, yet loud. With mine we listen to each other. Everyone waits for the person to speak before they start talking.

Ira Introduces Trevor

MAY 2003

It's a weekend that I'm in the New York area and because Ira wants me his friend Trevor. We're heading into the city from New Jersey to meet up with him.

As our relationship develops, it's becoming clear to me that Ira is close to his family and has a close-knit group of friends. If I'm going to meet Trevor, it must mean that he's important in Ira's life. Even though I haven't met Trevor yet, I have a feeling that he will be important in my life, too.

As we're driving into the city, I ask Ira, "Remind me how you know Trevor?"

Ira says, "It's kind of a long story."

I reply, "I got nothing but time here."

Ira begins weaving his tale:

"We were working for the same company. I was on the business development side and Trevor was on the technical support side. We were involved in a few deals but not really that close. He seemed to me to be a smart kid, but came across as a bit arrogant.

"Somehow, it came up that I live in Morristown. Trevor told me that his family has a country house in the neighboring town, Mendham and asked if I'd like to go out fishing on a boat in the pond at his house. I was thinking a lot of things all at the same time. First of all, I'm really not sure I like this guy. Second, who in the hell has a pond at their house that they can take a boat to fish? Third, what if the old 'fishing in the boat in my country home pond' is code for 'kill you and dump you in said pond'?"

We're on the 280 heading to the Holland Tunnel, and while Ira describes this to me, a girl who grew up in Jersey City where people don't have country homes, I'm beginning to see why he wasn't sure if he liked Trevor.

Ira continues. "I'm not sure what it was about the offer, or if it was just the insistence by Trevor, but I surprisingly agreed with this basically-unknown man on a boat in his pond at his country home." Ira fakes a news anchorman voice, "And in an unrelated story, a business development manager is still missing after accepting an offer to go fishing."

We both laugh but a little nervously.

Ira goes on.

"So Trevor has me meet him. We walk in and no one else is there. Trevor opens a coat closet and he throws me a life jacket and then hands me an oar. He grabs two fishing poles and a yellow tackle box. I look around the house. It is very well appointed and has a definite air of money and taste, but the decor is a throwback to the late '70s or early '80s. Trevor gets a six pack of beer, and slaps me on the back and says, 'Come on!'

"We head out the back door and I see the pond. Visions of my family and friends flash before my eyes. I try to silently tell my mom and dad that I love them, hoping that they can hear the voice in my head should this all go horribly wrong. Trevor heads to a wooden dock. It is worn and creaky and an upside rowboat rests on it.

"'Hey, give me a hand,' Trevor says, and we turn the boat right side up and put it in the water. He gets into the hull with the ease of someone who has done this a time or two.

"I get in not as gracefully.

"We head out around the lake. Trevor is expounding on the pond and the fishing he has done here as a kid and how it is a great thing that his family wanted to make sure that as a kid growing up in NYC he had the balance of a natural environment.

"We start to fish.

"Trevor's fishing line hits quick. This guy is good. Or maybe this pond is stocked. He hits again. This time it's an even bigger fish. I'm casting and casting. Nothing yet.

"Trevor cracks open a beer and we are just a couple of guys hanging out on a boat in the middle of this pond at his country home. It is pretty Norman Rockwell idyllic. Then it happens. In a moment of truth or some other cosmic confession, Trevor utters the words that I will never forget."

"What did he say?" I ask. I'm on the edge of the seat hoping that we hit some traffic so I can hear more of this story.

Ira smiles and returns to the story. "He says, 'I hate my job!'

"'Holy shit,' I say. 'I am so glad you said that. So do I!' We both laugh, and in that moment, a real friendship is forged."

We arrive in New York City and I meet the infamous Trevor. When I first see him, I think that he is not what I pictured. We get to meet and hang out and I can see he is the "larger than life" character that Ira describes.

The Non-Ask

MY SOLO-GIRL-OUT-IN-THE-WORLD TRIP IS FEELING A BIT compromised. I planned to go by myself. Just me. Out in the world. Without a care. Without a plan. Without an itinerary.

Cue Gwen Stefani's song, *Girl in the World*, to get the vibe of the bad-assery that I was putting down for this trip.

I had already envisioned the exotic places I would visit. I already had a sense of curiosity about the new people I would meet, both locals and fellow travelers. I decided that I would let these interactions shape where I was heading. My mental picture became clearer: I'm sitting in a cafe in India. The room is buzzing with activity. I'm sipping chai, backpack at my side, listening to the locals talk. I'm watching the scene of me being out in the world unfold in front of me.

But I'm starting to fall in love with Ira. Is going on this trip by myself really what I want to do?

Solo was the plan though. But that was the plan when I was dating a bunch of guys that weren't right for me. But is Ira "the one"? If I asked him to go, would he even uproot his entire life to go with me, would he follow me to the end of the earth? Around the world?

If I go on this trip by myself, do I risk losing him? If I ask him, do I risk losing the dream I planned for?

~

I'M IN A CAFE WITH IRA IN SAN FRANCISCO. HE HAS COME out to be with me for a few days. We've enjoyed our time together and it's nearly time for him to leave for his flight home.

I decide to put a feeler out there. I ask him in the most non-committal way I can, "Hey, if I ask you if you would want to come on the trip with me, what would you say? I'm not saying I am asking you, but if I did?"

"I would say, 'yes,'" Ira says.

I reiterate my lack of commitment. "Well, I'm not asking you, but it's good to know what you would say."

"I would say, 'yes,'" Ira repeats.

In case I missed it the first time.

Pros/Cons

JUNE 2003

I'M IN NYC ON THE UPPER WEST SIDE. WE HAVE TICKETS for a concert but have to arrive separately as Ira is coming from work. We're meeting at a restaurant before the show. I arrive at the restaurant earlier than we planned to meet, I sit at the bar, and order a drink. I do the thing I tend to do when I'm alone: write a pro /con list. Not having paper handy, I use the back of the menu and jot down these:

Pros of taking Ira on the trip:

- Shared memories.
- Shared expenses.
- Keep the love of my life close to me.

Cons of taking Ira on the trip:

- My plan of doing this trip solo is out the window.
- I'll have to account for another's thoughts/plans/desires.

I feel a presence looming near and look up from my task. Ira stands in front of me, jean jacket and all.

"Hi, babe," he says, giving me a kiss.

"Hi, babe," I reply, giving him another kiss.

"What are you writing?" he asks.

"A pro/con list of whether it makes sense to ask you to come with me on this trip."

He laughs. Amused yet tinged the tiniest bit with fear.

"What did you come up with?" he asks.

I hand him the list.

He reads it. And waits.

"Hey," he says.

"Hey," I reply.

We stare into each other's eyes.

The restaurant/bar seems to fade. There is nothing but the two of us.

"Want to come on a 'round the world trip with me?" I ask.

"I thought you'd never ask," he says.

"Is that a yes?" I ask.

"That's a hell yes!" he says.

We kiss and kiss and kiss.

Alrighty then. This is going to be a new thing.

The Wind

JUNE 2003

Ring.

Ring.

Ring.

My mom.

"I'm watching something on TV about India. You should watch it," she says.

"I'm not by a TV now, mom. How does India look?"

"It seems very windy. Make sure you are careful of the wind."

"Yeah, mom. I will be."

The Call

JUNE 2003

IRA AND I CONTINUE TRAVERSING THE UNITED STATES FOR our extended weekend dates. And then I get the call. The call that no one wants to get—especially when they are 3,000 miles away.

"Your dad is in the hospital," my mom says in between breaths.

"What happened?" I ask. "Can I talk to him?"

"It's his heart," my mom says.

It doesn't feel right to be hearing this while so far away. I feel so helpless. "I'll be on the next flight."

"You don't have to do that, sweetie. Let's see what the doctors say."

I go home to pack my bags.

Ring.

Ring.

Ring.

It's my mom.

"Maybe you should come home, sweetie."

I head to the airport. I let Deloitte know that my dad is sick and I'm going back to New Jersey. They are totally supportive and tell me to take as much time as I need.

I take the time. I move in with my parents to be close. The trip is no longer the top priority. Being there for my dad and my mom is the top priority. I take him to doctors appointments, run errands, watch hours of TV on the couch with my parents. My mom is "the rock" of the family staying strong for my dad. I stay for a few months, then he starts feeling a little better.

He encourages me to head back to San Francisco to get some of my things. "I'll be fine. See you when you get back," he says.

I head back to San Francisco to pack up some more clothes and get my car. My plan is to drive the car across the country so it will be with me in New Jersey.

Long, Far, Hard

AUGUST 2003

I ASK IRA IF HE WANTS TO JOIN ME ON THIS CROSS-COUNTRY road trip.

He happily accepts. What he doesn't realize when he accepts is that driving in a tiny roadster with the top down all the way is not going to be super comfy for him. He knew that was the plan, but it hadn't sunk in what this really means.

Top down, even through the desert.

Top down, even in the extreme heat.

Top down, even though the sun is blazing down on us.

Just a few days into our trip, we're in a gift shop when Ira gets a call from his friend Davie. Ira walks down a different aisle so he can have the conversation in private. What he doesn't realize is that I can still hear him.

"It's long. It's far. It's hard," he says to Davie.

We're only in Nevada.

We make it all the way to Tennessee with the convertible top down. We guzzle gallons of water, which leads to countless bathroom breaks. I take many photos of Ira pumping gas and squeegee-ing the windows.

And then it starts raining.

Hard. Biblical.

Up goes the convertible top as we're driving through the storms. It rains the whole time we're in Tennessee. And it is a wide state.

Ira is on a two-week vacation from work. We're singing along to a song on the radio when he gets a text from his boss asking if Ira can talk to him in two hours.

"What do you think he wants?" I ask.

"I'm not really sure," Ira replies.

"It's kind of odd that he wants to talk to you on your vacation," I say.

"I know," he says, with a worried tone in his voice.

We continue to drive through the pouring rain. In silence. Wondering. Imagining the news is not good news.

Ira is also on a fast track in his career and had risen to director level when we met. He is on the path to be a vice president. He is a likable guy, works his ass off, and is successful at what he does. Ira stays at this job even though he knows it isn't the best career for him, and things are not that great there. Sales are down, management berates employees. Tensions are high. He's sticking it out because he doesn't want to start something new when he knows he will be quitting soon to go on this trip. But staying in a soul-sucking job is taking its toll on Ira's health.

We plan to hit a stopping point when Ira needs to have this call with his boss. We find a place called Love's Truck Stop, and Ira gets me situated in a booth with coffee and something to eat.

He returns to the car to do the call. I feel bad for him that he has to go back out into the pouring rain. Also, what can be so important that it can't wait until he gets back from his vacation?

I want to be with him in the car, but I know he needs take this call by himself.

After what seems like hours, but that I know is really less than an hour, I see Ira running back into the restaurant. His jean jacket is soaked from the rain.

He sits down.

"What happened?" I ask.

"I got fired," he says.

"Oh, I am so sorry, babe."

"Yeah, the CEO said that things weren't working out and that it might be better if we parted ways."

"Parted ways? Sounds like something someone would say during a bad breakup," I say.

Ira tries to put on a brave face. "I gotta say that I am not getting any love here in Love's Truck Stop," he says.

I can tell that even though he has just been hanging on to this job until we leave for the trip, he is devastated.

At the same time, there's a piece of me that is glad that this chapter of his business career is over, and he can find a company that's a better fit and more humane to its employees.

We now have to focus on the fact that there has been a definite shift in this road trip. Instead of it being about relaxing and taking some time to enjoy a cross-country trip together, it's a somber race to get to New Jersey.

It's still pouring when we get back in the car. The noise of the rain hitting the convertible is so loud that I think it's going to rip a hole in the top.

It drowns out the silence between us.

Musical Chairs

I'M VISITING SAN FRANCISCO. I DECIDE IT'S TIME TO revisit my year sabbatical and book a meeting with my boss Mark. He invites me in at the appointed time, and I sit down opposite him. "Hey Mark."

"Hey Joanne. Come in."

I walk into his office and sit down opposite his desk.

"I wanted to let you know you did a great job at the client. They are really happy with the results of the project," he says.

"That's great to hear. I'm glad the client and everyone are happy. I think it's a good time to take that leave of absence I've been talking about."

"Well, I wanted to talk to you about that."

"Yeah?"

He breaks the news that our group is merging with another Deloitte group, and he'll no longer lead our team. He explains that he'll be fine—he's close to retirement anyway—but the restructuring could mean that there wouldn't be a place for me if I took off as planned. "But, But," I'm rendered incapable of putting sentences together.

"A few more months. It's going to be like musical chairs around here. And if you're up somewhere meditating on a mountain when the music turns off, there may not be a chair for you when you get back," he says.

"But, but…." I stammer until he jumps in.

"Here's what I would do. Stay until the restructuring is complete. Secure your spot. Then take your leave. I'd hate to see you lose everything you've worked so hard for."

BACK AT THE COSMOPOLITAN CAFE, I TELL MY FRIENDS what's happening at Deloitte and say that I'm thinking of staying a few more months.

One of my friends shakes his head and lets out a little *tssssk*.

"What was that for?" I ask while taking a big swig of my cosmopolitan.

"I don't think you're ever going on this trip. You're going to keep talking about it and delaying it. And it will never happen."

I start to protest.

He just looks at me with a knowing glance.

"Watch me. I'll make it," I say with as much confidence as I can muster. Although I'm not too sure that he isn't right.

Will I ever take this trip? Will something always happen that causes a delay?

New Jersey to San Francisco

2004

ALL THAT MATTERS AT THIS POINT IS TO BE WITH MY DAD
as he tries to get back to better health. Days become weeks. Weeks
become months. Time is spent between my parents' house and
visiting Ira at his house.

I'm on a family medical leave of absence from Deloitte. They are
supportive of me taking a break to spend time with my dad. There are
no work projects to distract me from being there for him. Ira and I
have gone from having two jet-setting careers to nothing. We're no
longer flying across the country to meet.

Real life sets in.

Doctors' visits.

Hospital visits.

Not exactly sure what we are doing with our lives. Our trip planning is on hold until my dad gets better.

Ira's friend and around the corner neighbor, Davie, tells Ira about a
job opening he saw in town at Sandrian Camera, a camera shop and
film development store that has been part of the town for close to
ninety years. Ira interviews with them, returning with a job offer.

"It's a part-time job, selling camera supplies to customers. Fifteen
bucks an hour, with some commissions."

"Are you going to feel okay working in a shop making just above minimum wage after your career in business development?" I ask.

"I don't want to take a full-time job when I know I'm going to be taking this trip," Ira says. "It wouldn't be right for any company to do that."

"But what about the camera shop?"

"I told them about the trip, and they said they'd be happy to have me work there part-time until I left."

"Well, that's good."

"I guess. I can't get this nagging conversation I've had with my dad over the years out of my head."

"What conversation is that?" I ask.

'Well, it was him that got me interested in photography as a kid, but he didn't want me to actually *pursue* it as a career. I mean, I know he worked his ass off as a company controller five days a week and then worked another job on the weekends to afford to pay for my college. When I was deciding on what to do after college, *my plan* was to go to Santa Barbara. There is a great photo school there. I was going to learn to surf and to photograph."

"But you went for your MBA instead?"

"Yeah, in a godfatheresque-way my dad made me *an offer I couldn't refuse*: to pay for my MBA. He told me, 'Get your MBA and you will always have it to fall back on.' I also think that he hoped that getting my MBA would get the *fakakta* idea of being a photographer out of my head."

"*Fakakta*? What is that?"

Ira remembers that I am Catholic and not fluent in Yiddish.

"*Fakakta* is a Yiddish word meaning a shitty or crappy idea. It can also describe a thing, an object or a person that is completely messed up, which is what I believe my dad had in mind about my idea to be a photographer."

Ira also shares that when he first told his dad that he wanted to be a photographer, his dad's response was, "What are you going to do? Take pictures of babies at the Sears portrait studio in the mall?" He wanted bigger things for his son.

"But, babe," I say, "There are bigger things for you than taking photos of babies. I know it." Then I add, "And getting your MBA has been very good for you."

Ira knows this and we are both silent for a moment.

I continue, "Will you be happy working there?"

"You know I've wanted to break into photography as a career. Maybe this will get me closer."

"You should do it then."

And in the time it takes for a shutter to click, Ira goes from negotiating hundred-million-dollar deals in a global arena to selling cameras in a local camera shop.

I admire Ira for being able to adjust so willingly to this downgrading of his stature, leaving the pumped-up business world, and for choosing to focus on finding his happiness by trying to become a photographer.

A big added bonus is that he won't have a monster of a boss yelling at him.

"JOANNE, WHY DON'T YOU TAKE THAT TRIP YOU'VE BEEN talking about? Life is short," my dad says as we are sitting on the couch in his living room.

"But dad, I want to be here with you while you are getting better."

"I am doing better. My last visit to my doctor he said he was really impressed with my recovery."

"Yeah, but," I protest.

"If you don't go now, I don't want it to be my fault. I want you to go."

"Will you be okay?" I ask, knowing that no one really knows the answer to this.

"I'm going to be fine. Really."

And with that I call Deloitte to find out what the next steps should be.

"Mark, how is it going there?"

"Lots of changes. How's your dad?" he says.

"He's doing much better. Thanks for asking. That's kind of why I'm calling."

"Oh?" he asks

"Well, he is doing much better and feels good about me taking the trip," I say.

Silence.

"I plan to be back in San Francisco next week and I figured I'd come in to talk with you about all the details."

"You've been out of work for a long time. Lots has changed here."

"Yeah, I've heard about some of the changes. What does it mean for me?"

"Well, I'm not the one to approve your leave of absence anymore. You'll have to talk to the new partner."

"Oh, I don't know her at all. What's she like?"

"Schedule a meeting with her assistant and let me know what you think."

So, with that non-answer, I say goodbye and make another call to schedule my meeting.

"HI JOANNE. GREAT TO MEET YOU. I'VE HEARD LOTS ABOUT you."

I'm back in San Francisco, sitting in the office of Ms.-new-partner-in-charge. I want to make the standard joking reply "All good, I hope?" but she doesn't seem to be in a joking mood.

"Thanks."

Words are not forming.

"So, what is this I hear about wanting to take a leave of absence to travel?"

"Umm, yes, well. I'm really committed to staying with Deloitte and trying to make partner and I thought it would be a good idea to take a break before that process begins."

"Right. Well, if we give you this leave of absence, I need you to do a few things."

"Sure, what things?"

"Well, for one, you will be gone during our annual review process. We would need you to dial in to talk through how the people who worked for you did during the year."

"I know that's a two-day meeting. Will I be able to dial in and give the feedback on all of the team members all at once?"

"No, you know that's not how it works, Joanne. They'll be spread out over the two days, so we would expect you to be there the whole time. Dialing in, of course."

I imagine my long-distance phone bill. I imagine being on top of a mountain in Bhutan with the stress of trying to get reliable cell phone coverage. I imagine being in the desert of India in a windstorm. I imagine the time zone differences and being awake all night.

"And another thing," she says. "You've already had a lot of time off, and this vacation added on to it will be more."

"The recent time off was to be with my dad while he was sick," I say. "It was a family medical leave."

"Yes, yes, I know. But we expect when you come back that you will hit it out of the park here. So, I want you to keep in touch with some of the partners and position yourself, so you get another project right away when you get back. You will need to sell yourself."

Calling in from the mountaintop.

Selling myself.

Hitting it out of the park.

"But the whole point of this trip is to take a break. And reduce my stress. This all sounds pretty stressful," I say.

"Well, this is what you need to do to take this leave of absence."

Silence.

"Unless...."

She trails off in deep thought. "Unless you just leave and then you won't have to do any of this. And when you're done traveling, you can come back. You'd have to reapply, but it would be more of a formality.

With your record prior to this year of absences, you have a good record."

Ten years. Ten years of climbing up the ladder. "Making it" at Deloitte. Poof! All gone.

But dialing in from the mountaintop seems ridiculous. And I definitely don't feel like "hitting it out of the park." I know that having me "on the books" of her team but not bringing in any revenue is probably dragging down her numbers. Reading between the lines, I can see that she is hoping I'll take the second option. I think about all this for a moment more. Then I say, "I'll take you up on the offer to leave."

She says that someone in HR will reach out to me.

We say our goodbyes.

As I walk past the cubicles toward the parking lot, my head spins, but I think I've taken the better of the two options.

I feel free.

I'm scared yet relieved. Now it's time to plan our trip. I've thought about adventure for so long. Is it finally going to happen?

The Plan

MY DAD IS DOING BETTER. IRA AND I ARE DONE WITH OUR jobs. Now we just need to decide exactly where we are going. What began as just and extended trip to Thailand has turned into more countries. Lots more. Why not turn it into a round-the-world trip? The plan is to stay in less expensive countries to make our dollars last longer.

Ira has his list of "must do" countries. I have mine. Some we agree on. Some we don't. We stick pins on a map and figure out our route. We negotiate. Some countries are dropped; others are added.

In the end, we have a rough idea of which countries make the list.

I would have never picked Russia, but that's a country Ira really wants to see.

Ira would have never picked India, but that's a country I want to see. And now I can tell my mom that Ira will be there to protect me from the wind.

We both leave our negotiations feeling good about what we landed on. It doesn't feel one-sided. We both feel like the other's voice was heard.

I guess this is what a true relationship is about.

Leaving, Leaving, Leaving?

MARCH 2005

WE'RE FINALLY SCHEDULED AND HAVE TICKETS FOR OUR first stop: Tokyo, Japan. It's past midnight and we're scrambling to finish lots of last-minute stuff like mail forwarding, bill auto pay, and such. Finally, we're all tucked in, exhausted, and about to get a few hours of sleep before our early morning flight from Newark International Airport.

"Babe, have you seen the iPod?" Ira asks.

I reply with my standard answer when trying to figure out where any lost item is, "Where did you see it last?" We laugh because we know this is a ridiculous question, since we just moved everything from the first floor of the house to the second floor in order to rent the first floor while traveling.

"It might be in my 4Runner in the garage," Ira says.

"Why don't you check in the morning and let's get some sleep now?" I say.

"I'm not going to be able to sleep without knowing where it is."

I get it. It's loaded with all our favorite travel songs and we've envisioned listening to it on long flights and train rides.

Ira leaves the house to head down the long driveway to check out his 4Runner which is safely tucked into our detached garage.

About twenty minutes later he returns, a pained look on his face.

"What happened to you, babe?" I ask.

"I fell on the outside stairs. You know that spot where the gutter drips water? Well, it turned into ice," Ira says. "I've been on my back looking up at the stars, wondering how I'm going to tell you that I don't think I will be able to get on a twenty-hour flight. I think I pulled a disc or something serious. You may have to go without me."

"What? Go without you?

"I don't see another way. You can start out and I'll meet you when I'm better."

"Let's get you some ice and figure this out," I say.

We look at each other and realize that there is no ice because of the shuffle of the house.

"I know what to do, let's use some snow," I say.

I scoop snow from the balcony off our bedroom. Is this going to be a solo trip after all? I can't leave without him.

"I'm not going to go on the trip alone and leave you here hurt," I say.

"I'm not going to let you miss your flight," Ira says. He knows we booked a non-refundable/non-transferable fare for this first leg of the trip in order to save money. There's no way we'll miss this flight, we'd thought.

"Do you think you need to go to the ER?" I ask.

"No, I think the ice, umm snow, is helping. Let's get some sleep and figure it out in the morning," he says.

We're exhausted from the day and drift off to sleep not knowing what the morning will bring. I dream of planes and ice and missed connections.

We wake up to a blizzard.

We call the airline to say that due to the snow we're not sure if we can make it to the airport, hoping they will shift our flight with no penalty. We also realize that this would give Ira's back another day to heal.

The airline agrees that due to the blizzard, the flight is most likely going to be cancelled. They locate the same flight departing tomorrow, and transfer our reservations without penalty.

We can breathe a bit deeper. We've got an extra day. Ira rests his back. We go to his chiropractor. He takes it easy.

And at the end of the day, Ira says, "I think I can make the flight."

I'm relieved not only because he's going to be okay, but because I'm not sure I can handle one more setback about this trip.

Japan: Man of the Quarter

MARCH 2005

WE FLY TO TOKYO, JAPAN, WHERE WE'RE PLANNING TO STAY with our friends, Sabina Yoon and Chris Moore, and their new baby, Alyssa. Chris and I worked together at Deloitte and he's now an expat living in Japan. They've offered for us to stay in their extra room. Having an extra bedroom is not a common thing in Japan, where space is a luxury. But since they just had a baby, his company upgraded them to a two-bedroom apartment.

It's in a luxury skyscraper right in the heart of the downtown area, with breakfast provided every day.

Since Alyssa still sleeps in their room, the extra room can become our home while we're in Japan.

On the flight, Ira shares with me some things about his former project in Japan.

"Have I told you that I made Man of the Quarter when I worked on that project?"

"Man of the Quarter? What were you doing for the other nine months?" I joke.

He seems a bit hurt by my joke.

I backpedal. "No, just kidding. Tell me more about it."

"Because of my contribution to our Japanese office, I was given their Man of the Quarter award, which was only given to someone that was not Japanese one other time. Out of 11,000 people," he says.

"Eleven thousand people? Wow, that is insane!" I say. "How did you get it?"

"I worked on this deal to sell Nippon Telegraph and Telephone $100 million of computer equipment for a Real Time Telephone Network. It took three years to complete the deal and I traveled to Japan about six times in the course of moving this forward. I tried to read everything I could, Japanese business etiquette books, and I even got Japanese language training because I wanted to have a way to communicate with and understand my counterparts and the client better."

"Three years? That's a long time," I say. "But it sounds like it was a cool project. Did you say $100 million?"

"Yeah, it was huge for my company. And going through the process of the sale and developing the friendships with my Japanese counterparts was pretty life-changing."

"And we are going to meet with two of the guys in Tokyo, right?"

"Yeah, Kono-san and Onishi-san."

Ira is very excited that as part of the trip he will get the opportunity to be back in Japan and to see his friends.

"Kono-san is a guy that you just have to love, he has a great wide smile. He was from our company's Japan office but living in the San Francisco area. He was on assignment to be the Japanese liaison manager for business between other countries and the Japan office. He is fluent in both Japanese and English, but more importantly he was an enormous help in navigating between the two cultures."

"Sounds like an awesome role," I say. "Did you guys have fun while in Japan or was it all work?"

"Oh, we had fun. I remember that we were out one night in Tokyo and we were at a karaoke bar which is a really big deal for Japanese businessmen. I was very nervous about getting up and singing in front of the others from the project, but Kono-san leaned over to me and said, 'Ira-san, this is a form of trust. The Japanese businessman is very serious about their work. Karaoke is one of the only times that they get to express themselves. If you do not sing, they will wonder about your character and may not trust you.'"

"What did you do?" I ask.

"I sang, but I have to be honest, I think I really could have picked a better song."

"What was it?"

"Bob Marley's *No Woman, No Cry.*"

We both laugh.

"Tell me about the other guy."

"Onishi-san was the more serious one of the two, or so it seemed. He was my main contact at the Japanese office. Over the course of the three years, we spent many hours on the phone, in email, and singing karaoke when I was in Japan.

"There is a memory of Onishi-san thst I will never forget. After the deal was completed and the hardware was shipped to Japan, I got notified that I had been named Man of the Quarter. I got to fly over to accept the award. Onishi-san and I had a day or two of business meetings before the award ceremony. We took a train ride to Kamakura to do some touristy things. On the train ride back, I told Onishi-san, 'I have a sketch of an acceptance speech. But I have one problem.'"

"'What is it, Ira-san? How can I help?'

"I would like to show my appreciation for this award, and I would like to give the speech in Japanese."

"'Really?' he responded and then he gave me a respectful wink.

"I told Onishi-san that I wanted to say, 'I thank you from the bottom of my heart.'

"I told him the next line, and then he said, 'Ira-san, no translation.' I took this to mean that we would need to come up with something similar but not really change the context.

"We spent the next hour and a half on the train, with me telling him I want to say this and he's trying to find the best way to say it in Japanese.

"I remember the leather seats we were sitting on next to each other going back and forth on the translations. I remember actually pausing a moment while he was searching to find the best way to say one of my lines in my speech."

"That sounds like a great memory. How were you feeling at the time?"

"I looked at him and I just thought, how did I get to be so lucky to be here? I am traveling on a train from Kamakura to Tandem Japan's Tokyo office, where I will be given the Man of the Quarter award. This has only happened a few times in my life where, when the moment was happening, I could step outside of it and realize how insanely amazing that experience was. And know that it was very rare."

Ira pulls out a photo.

"I brought this to show them," he says. It's a picture of him, Onishi-san, and Kono-san standing all in business suits and ties in front of the NT&T office building in Japan. The photo is shot from a set of lower steps and they are on steps above, so they look larger than life. They look like a trio of young badass sales guys that had just closed a huge deal, which they had.

"I can't wait to meet them!" I say.

"I can't wait until they meet you," Ira says. He smiles.

I think that asking Ira to come on this trip might have been a good idea. He is someone who really enjoys exploring new cultures with a sense of respect and inquisitiveness, and who loves forging friendships.

We arrive in Japan. Our first stop. It sinks in that the trip has finally started.

After all this time of starting and stopping, of planning and not planning, of wondering whether this trip was going to happen. And now it has.

It's great that we have somewhere free to stay with friends. We hit the early morning fish market, the giant Buddha, took an overnight trip to Kyoto, and enjoyed many amazing meals.

～

TOWARDS THE END OF OUR STAY, WE FINALLY MEET ONISHI-san and Kono-san. They have a brief break in their workday and meet us in a hotel bar over the lunch hour. They live up to the stories. And maybe even surpass the stories. Their personalities are larger than life. I get to hear about Ira when he was the hot shot sales guy. Making big deals. Making lifelong friends. Making everyone laugh at his karaoke singing.

Now I can see why Ira kept in touch with these guys. I can tell how much respect they have for each other. And how tight their friendship was.

"What are you doing now, Ira-san?" Kono-san asks.

"Well, I'm pursuing my dream to become a photographer," Ira responds. "I have a few more days in Japan and I'm hoping to get some photos of something unique," he says.

"Good for you, Ira-san. I will think about this," Onishi-san says. "We only wish the best for you."

"And what about you, Joanne?" Onishi-san asks.

"I previously worked at Deloitte Consulting, but I left to take this trip. I'm going to try writing some stories about our travels," I say.

They look confused.

"Deloitte is a good career. Will you go back there?"

"I'm not sure, taking it a day at a time on this trip," I say.

There is silence. I read into this silence that this is something they would not consider doing with their careers.

"Why don't you meet us for dinner tonight?" Kono-san asks.

I look at Ira. I can tell he wants to say yes but knows we have plans with my friends Sabina and Chris.

I jump in.

"Babe, why don't you go to dinner with your friends and I'll go with my friends. I know you have lots to catch up on."

"Are you sure?" Ira says.

"Yes, definitely," I say

Later that night, Ira explained the scene of what happened with Kono-san and Onishi-san. It went like this:

"Ira-san, do you want some shochu?" Onishi-san asks.

"What's shochu?"

"Ahh, Ira-san, you will try and see."

After a few sips of shochu, Ira is really liking this drink.

"How come I've never heard of this?" Ira asks.

Kono-san explains that shochu has traditionally been more of a worker's drink, but is starting to come into its own as a higher-end drink.

"It's the next big thing," Onishi-san says. "You told me that you and Joanne want to take photos and write about something different in Japan. This is it."

"I'd love to learn more about the drink," Ira says.

"I have a friend on the island of Kyushu who makes Shochu. I will call him and see if he can get you into their plant. I will let them know you are a photographer from New York and to let you in."

"Oh, that is great. We still have a few days left in Japan," Ira says.

"You will need more time than that."

Ira returns to what feels like our apartment now that we've been here close to two weeks.

"How was your dinner with Onishi-san and Kono-san?" I ask.

"It was great," Ira says. "And well, they told me about another stop in Japan we must do."

"Oh, cool. We still have two days left here before we head to New Zealand," I say.

"Yeah, well the issue is that it's on an island and we'd have to fly there."

"Fly there?"

"Yeah, it's pretty far from here," Ira says.

"But our next flight to New Zealand is in two days."

"Yeah, I don't know if we can make that."

"How important is this stop to you?"

"They said it was the next big thing."

"Well, if that's true, let's do it," I say. "We did buy tickets with dates that could be changed just in case something like this happens. I love not being tied to a schedule."

And just like that, we're heading to Kagoshima, on the island of

Kyushu. This is where the shochu is made. Shochu is like the working-man's sake.

The idea is that we will research a story about this "next big thing" drink. Ira will take the pictures and I will write about it.

We spend the day touring the facilities of Komasa Shochu, which is the connection we made through Onishi-san. Over the course of the day, we become friends with the owner, and we end up being invited to dinner with his family. The restaurant that they take us to has all pork items on the menu.

Every. Single. Item.

But the food is all amazing. And such a variety of dishes. I never knew pork could be made into so many things.

When we get to dessert, they serve us lemon sorbet. I try the sorbet and it doesn't taste like lemon. I must have an odd look on my face.

"Pork. Pork," the mom says.

I then realize what she means. Even the ice cream is made out of pork. I smile. I don't eat much of the dessert after that.

South Island, New Zealand: Is The Baby in the Trunk?

MARCH 2005

BANG! BANG!

Bang!

"Right, you need to leave and pay your bill. Are you coming round now?" I hear someone on the other side of the door say.

"Isn't checkout at eleven?" I yell back, through the door.

"No, it's ten!" they yell back.

"Oh. Just a few more minutes," I yell as I'm cramming stuff in my backpack.

This is not the welcoming New Zealand we saw in the brochure—but then we look at that brochure and realize it's clearly stated that checkout is at 10 AM sharp.

We are in Noah's Ark backpackers. Backpackers is the hip name the Kiwis have for hostels. Every room here is done in a different animal theme. We are in the giraffe room. Giraffes are painted everywhere.

Last night, as we were lying in the bunk-bed with the giraffe theme, falling into a dream state, Ira looked at me and said, "Not as comfortable as the Heavenly Bed."

Ahhh, the Westin. I miss staying there. I miss the Heavenly Bed. I miss the room service bringing me breakfast. I miss the expense account.

But I don't miss the work that went along with the fancy hotels. "So true," I said as I fell asleep dreaming of giraffes.

Bang! Bang! Bang!

Back to reality.

"We're leaving now," Ira says through the door.

We rush out to our car—it's a Toyota something, with over 100,000 miles--which we're planning on driving straight across the island to visit the Franz Joseph Glacier.

Ira goes to start it and the engine does not turn over.

"What's going on?" I ask.

"Oh, shoot. I must've left the lights on," Ira says.

"Didn't the car warn you that the lights were on?"

Ira explains that since the car is an older model, it did not give the usual "Hey buddy, you have your lights on" when he turned off the engine.

"Not a problem," I say. "We'll just get a jump start and be on our way."

We go back to Noah's Ark to tell them what happened.

"I don't own a car," the front desk attendant says. "But there's a car painting shop just across the street. Maybe they could get you right."

We head over and find a man who is engrossed in his work of painting and polishing a car. Ira asks if he might be able to help a poor American down on his luck and in need of a jump for the battery.

The painter is extremely understanding, stops his work, and produces a full jump start kit. Then we all head over to the car, he opens the hood and hooks up wires to things under the hoods of our car. Then he tells Ira "Hit it on the gunny."

Ira turns the key and the car turns over. Hurrah! We are back to the plan of soaking up New Zealand.

We've been driving on a long, straight road for about an hour, with nothing to see but small animals like jackrabbits, tumbleweeds and lots of open spaces, when Ira suddenly has a pained look on his face.

"What's going on?" I say.

"I'm not sure if all of my camera equipment is in the trunk," he says.

"We did a sweep through the place when we were leaving. I don't remember seeing any camera equipment," I say. "But you can check. Just don't turn the car off because I don't think the battery is fully charged."

"That's the problem," Ira says.

"Huh?"

"The trunk is only able to be opened by the key."

Oh.

I know that if he doesn't check, he will be miserable for the entire ride across the country. "Well, if you have to check to see if you have your equipment, you have to check."

"Really?" he says.

"Yeah, just let's go to a gas station so if the car doesn't start, we will have an easier time getting a jump start compared to being out here in the middle of nowhere."

A few miles later we see a gas station. Ira looks at me as if to seal our fate and get my endorsement.

I nod.

Ira parks near the gas station, turns the key off, and heads for the trunk.

He heads back into the car and tells me what I already know. "The equipment was there," he says shyly. "I touched it to be sure."

Ira turns the key, and the engine makes a sound like it wants to try to start but really needed to be driven longer to have a half of a prayer. Ira tries one more time, and the engine emits that same tinny noise that does not resemble a car on the way to starting. He looks at me and says, "Well, at least we're in a gas station."

Ira takes charge of the situation that he got us into. He heads to the counter and again apologizes for everything he has done in his life that has brought him to this exact spot and for having to ask for help.

"No worries, mate," is the attendant's response. He also has a self-contained jump kit. We give it a go, but it is not powerful enough to start the old rental that we have.

We spend the next half hour asking everyone that comes into the gas station if they have "jumper leads," as they are called in New Zealand. The problem is that most of the people that we see are also in rental cars.

If they came with "jumper leads," we would not be in this situation.

Everyone that we ask is extremely nice and considering that we are stuck, it's a good experience meeting the New Zealanders that are trying to help us out. Finally, one guy has a pair of leads in the back of his truck and pulls around to our car and gives it a go.

It starts!

He advises us to run the car for an hour or so to recharge it. For the rest of the day, whenever we stop to see a sight, we leave the car running—just in case.

New Zealand: Matching Socks

MARCH 2005

WHEN WE ARE IN CHRISTCHURCH, ON THE SOUTH ISLAND of New Zealand, we go into the retail store of the New Zealand's Men's National Rugby Team, the "All Blacks." We tell them we are enjoying traveling around their country.

They give us ONE sock.

Black and White stripes. And tell us that if we go to the other store in Auckland, on the North Island, they will give us the other sock to match.

So when we go to Auckland a couple of weeks later, which was next on the itinerary, Ira gets the other sock.

Such a great marketing ploy to get you to go to the other store.

We play along.

Auckland, New Zealand: Dragon Boats Again

MARCH 2005

"YOU KNOW THAT ICEBREAKER GAME WHERE YOU HAVE TO say two truths and one lie about yourself, and then folks need to guess which one is the lie?" I ask Ira.

"Yeah, I know that one. Why do you ask?" he replies.

"Well, I always win at that," I say. "Because I say that I was a dragon boat racer who competed internationally."

"And no one guesses that as the truth?" Ira asks.

"Nope. One look at me, and no one thinks I can do that," I say. "I'm not sure if I should be excited that I won the game or bummed that no one thinks I'm strong enough to paddle a dragon boat. I paddled in Taipei, Taiwan. And I can't wait to add New Zealand to that list," I say. When I heard there was going to be a dragon boat race in Auckland, I knew I had to go!

I've been to so many races where a team was short a paddler, and they requested random paddlers to join their team for the race. I was hoping that when we got to the race in Auckland, a team would be short a paddler, and there would be a request like, "Is there a doctor in the house?" But it would be, "Is there a paddler on the dock?"

I would jump up and say, "I am! I'm Joanne Flynn from San Francisco, and I paddle on the AquaAssassins!"

There would be much rejoicing and high-fiving. And I would get to have this experience, adding more fuel for my icebreaker question.

The problem was that no team needed paddlers. They all had plenty of extras. I walked by each team to ask. They all said some form of "Sorry, mate."

While I searched for a team that needed a paddler, Ira somehow convinced the pacer boat that he should be let on to photograph the teams.

I was part of the crowd of people there to watch the race. I shimmied in to get close to the railing to get a good look. While I watch from the sideline, there he is out on the water. Not with a paddle but with his camera.

Smiling from ear to ear.

Tasmanian Devils

MARCH 2005

WE ARE IN SYDNEY, AUSTRALIA, WITHOUT A CLUE WHERE we are heading next. Great Barrier Reef? Ayers Rock? Melbourne?

I wanted to do the trip this way, to "figure it out as we go" to keep with the free-spirited nature I'd dreamt up. Sometimes this approached has worked. Other times, well, it's been a bit overwhelming. Australia is a large country with so many options.

To add to the importance of our next move, Easter is approaching and basically the whole country shut down. As I'm looking at the *Lonely Planet* guidebook, I have a crazy idea.

"Babe, what if we just went to Tasmania?" I ask Ira. "And skip the Great Barrier Reef."

"Tasmania? Wait, what?" Ira says.

"Yeah, I was reading that you can drive completely around the island. And, ya know, see Tasmanian devils," I say.

"What about the Great Barrier Reef? Can you really come to Australia and not see that?" Ira says. "Will they let us back in the US if we missed out?"

"Tasmanian devils," I remind Ira.

He looks at me and says, "Are you sure you want to do this?"

"Yeah, it'll be a blast. I'm sure of it."

And just like that we have flights to Tasmania.

Around Tasmania in a Campervan

APRIL 2005

THE PLACE WHERE WE ARE STAYING IS ABOUT A MILE AND A half away from downtown Hobart, which is the capital city of Tasmania. Not such a far walk. But it's straight uphill from the town to our bed and breakfast.

For a few nights we've explored Hobart and walked up the hill straight back to our place.

Every night—straight up the hill. Then the night comes when I ask Ira, "Why don't we take another way home?" I want to see something different on the walk back

"What's wrong with the way we know? It's a straight path," Ira says.

"Yeah, I know all about the shortest distance between two points is a straight line and all. But I'd like to try a different way back," I say.

"Babe, it's pretty late. Don't you want to just head back?"

"Let's just go up the road next to our road. And then cut over. How far of a diversion could that be?" I know we're walking around on an unknown street, in an unknown town, on an unknown continent. "It's just one block over."

We start up a different road that is clearly taking us in the same direction as our bed and breakfast. I feel satisfied. While we walk, we talk about our day, what our plans are for tomorrow, and what a good idea it was that we came to Tasmania. And then we look up. In front of us is a rock formation with no way to pass. We've dead-ended ourselves.

Um, what now?

We scramble around to see if there is any way to pass. Unpassable. We stand in complete darkness with nothing familiar around us.

"Maybe we should have taken the way we know," I admit. "What do we do now?"

"We head back down the hill," Ira replies calmly.

We turn around and walk back down the long road, retracing the steps we just made.

"We should have taken the way we know, " I admit again.

As much as in that moment Ira could have said, "I told you so," Ira is not an "I-told-you-so" kind of guy.

We find our "regular" street. I plodded along dejectedly back up the hill. Oh man, I really messed this one up.

When we arrive safely at our place, Ira says, "Babe, next time, can we take the way we know?"

"Sure can," I reply.

With just a vague idea of where we may stop along the way, we take off to go clockwise around the island of Tasmania. We see lots of flora and fauna. The road is narrow and appears to be even more narrow because our campervan is the biggest vehicle we have ever ridden in. The camper van has everything we need for our exploration: a small bed, a burner, a tiny refrigerator. As we're driving, I hear a little crinkle-crinkle coming from the driver's seat. I look over to see Ira pop something in his mouth.

"Hey, what's that?" I ask.

"What's what?" Ira replies.

"That thing you just popped into your mouth."

"Oh, it's just chocolate," he says.

After a year and a half of dating Ira, I realize that he is truly a chocoholic and always has some little morsel readily available.

Thailand: Soaked at Songkran

APRIL 2005

WHEN WE REACH BANGKOK, THE BUDDHIST NEW YEAR festival, Songkran, is going on in full force. The festival feels like one-part running of the bulls, one part New Year's Eve in Times Square, and two parts sheer insanity. It's a three-day national holiday that involves water, clay, and some spirituality—and it pretty much shuts down the entire country.

Our hotel appears to be the epicenter of the festival. When I booked this hotel, I made sure to look for one just off Khao San Road, a fun, but busy, street I remembered from my last visit as the main street where all the backpackers stayed. I thought I was being smart, positioning us close to, but not in the middle of, the action. I completely overlooked that our visit coincides with Songkran.

The Thai believe that smearing chalk, clay, and water on others during the festival will wash away evil spirits. This practice turns the streets of Bangkok into one huge water fight and clay-dousing event.

It is 11 in the morning, on our first full day in Bangkok, and there is an absolute scene happening on the street right outside our hotel. From our third floor window, we witness the madness unfolding.

Crowds of men and women walk with pans containing a mixture of water and clay. They smear the clay onto the faces of strangers who pass them. Some applications are a gentle smear on someone's cheek, while others completely squash another's face in the clay mixture that ranges from watery to the consistency of quick-dry cement.

The other festival ritual to attract good luck includes an act of showering passersby with water. Everyone from little children to older women and men spray people with anything from small water pistols to enormous super soakers. Luck overfloweth.

"Let's get out there and check it out," I say.

The scene below our window has ballooned in size. We gingerly approach the front of the hotel and step outside. I decide to buy a saucer and some clay and get in the mix of things. Ira has a clear plastic shield for his camera covering his head and shoulders as well as his camera. He looks like he is wearing a half-body shower curtain.

I'm gently applying the clay on the cheeks of others. Some follow my lead and gently apply some clay to my face. Suddenly, someone decides to take it up a notch and smears the mixture across my entire face and hair. Before long, I'm covered in clay. It feels exhilarating. I don't have a care in the world. Well, except wondering if the clay will easily wash out of my hair.

I'm laughing and enjoying the experience. I'm also thankful that I have a shower-curtained bodyguard. Ira's smile indicates he is having a blast photographing the chaos.

Ira moves to get closer to the crowd, and he and his plastic shield head for another area seeking photographic opportunities. I remain in the main square near a guy with a water hose who is soaking the crowd and a DJ who is spinning music that has everyone outside our hotel dancing and jamming.

I glance over at Ira and he's grinning like a schoolboy, clearly immersed in the moment and capturing the images for posterity. I think about my decision to invite him and I'm glad I did. I'm falling deeper in love with this guy. I can feel that the memories we have will last a lifetime. Our lifetime. Together. I can see spending the rest of our lives together. He shows up in different ways than other boyfriends (or is it boy-fiends?) I've had. No one in the past has made me feel as safe and protected as he does.

After getting soaked throughout the day, we agree that we need some protection and purchase two water guns. They are somewhere between the small water pistols and the super soakers. They will at least enable us to hold our own against most attacks.

Later in the day, we notice a temple nearby and try to seek some Songkran asylum there. It is calm compared to the scene just outside the temple walls, presenting a very powerful juxtaposition: people with clay on their faces in soaking wet clothes, kneeling in front of a statue of the Buddha and praying.

We join in and say some prayers of our own.

"What did you pray for?" Ira asks.

"Good things for us and for those that we know," I say. "What about you?"

"I prayed to make it back to our hotel safely."

I look at Ira with a quizzical glance.

"I should have prayed harder," he says.

Just as we are leaving the safety of the temple, with our clothes somewhat dry again from the afternoon sun, Ira gets blasted by a little boy, who is no more than five, with a water gun. Despite his young age, he is a great shot and gets Ira directly in the eye and ear.

Ira turns to fire back. The kid's mom squirts Ira as well. Now it is a family thing. They continue squirting each other and just having fun. The boy is relentless, hiding behind the wall outside the temple for cover and shooting.

And now I'm the one photographing.

The next day Ira decides to leave his camera and hard drives in the safe in the hotel and we head out for a while.

"It seems tamer today," Ira says.

"Not sure if it's good luck to say that," I reply.

Another traveler has told me about an area that is supposed to be less chaotic, and we make our way there. Things seem to be fine, except that I notice that people have gone from using water pistols to buckets. They fill the buckets from a vat of water stationed on the side of the road. Crowds of young boys hover and wait for people, just to drench them in good luck.

We realize that our water guns are no match for this pack of boys with buckets and that we have a problem. Ira rushes to charge them in an effort to create a diversion so they will leave me alone. It works. But he is now being chased by a pack of Thai boys, each of them with a pail of water against his little water gun. Ira ducks behind a mango cart. One of them reminds me of one of my former co-workers. He wore dark black glasses and had a serious but mischievous look.

I'm watching from the sideline as Ira tries to run away. He heads in one direction, but his shower sandals decide that they're not going to make the trip. Now, he's running shoe-less down a street in Bangkok with a pack of kids chasing him. Ira's dodging where he can. His face shows mixed emotions: fear combined with fun. There are vendors with street carts selling food, with wafts of delicious smells of spices permeating the air.

Joanne and Ira smeared with clay at the Songkan Festival (Bangkok, Thailand).
Photo credit: Ira L. Black

Ira turns back to retrieve his shoes when the first wave of water hits him. He tries to run but one of his Nike plastic shower sandals with the swoosh across the top winds up lodged around his calf. He's running as fast as he can, with a look of determination. I'm on the other side of the road, safe and dry. I catch his eye. We both start cracking up laughing.

I have to remember to tell my mom that he is protecting me not only from the wind but also from getting soaked.

WE LEAVE THE MADNESS OF BANGKOK BEHIND AND TRAVEL to the hilltop town of Chiang Mai. We have a week before we need to return to Bangkok to catch our flight to Bhutan, which is plenty of time to check out Chiang Mai. The only thing we're concerned about is our visas to India. With the festival, government offices are closed, delaying us acquiring the needed visas—and we have to have the visas in hand for a period of time before we can travel to India.

While we are checking out flights in a travel shop on Khao San Road, we notice that they provide a visa service.

"Why don't we have the travel agent get our Indian visas while we keep traveling?" I suggest to Ira.

"Are you sure it's going to be okay? We need to get the visas before we head to Bhutan so we can fly to India afterwards," Ira reminds me.

"Yeah, this is a service they provide. It says it right in their window. Let's do it," I say.

So we plan for Sook, the travel agent wearing a floral top, to get our visas while we head to Chiang Mai. But there is something we don't realize: she needs our passports to process the visas.

"You want us to leave our passports with you while we head to Chiang Mai?" Ira says.

"Yes, sir. The only way for us to get your visas for India is if you leave your passport here," Sook replies.

"Is there any other way?" I ask. "I thought we could leave a copy." We know it's a cardinal rule of travel to never let one's passport out of one's possession.

"No, this is the only way. Leave your passports with me and I will get your visas. No problem," she says.

Ira and I look at each other, uncertain of what to do.

Ira pulls me aside, "What if we come back and our passports are gone? How will we then get out of Bangkok to make our trip to Bhutan?"

"I don't think we have much of a choice," I say. "We have to trust." We leave our passports with Sook and hope that all the Songkran good luck we were doused with holds.

We head to Chiang Mai and explore all that there is in the misty mountains of Thailand. We see colorful hill tribes and temples galore.

Back on Khao San Road in Bangkok, Sook returned our passports. She realized that, due to the closures for the Thai New Year, she would not get our passports back in time if she sent them away to get our visas for India. And she didn't want us to miss our Bhutan trip.

We didn't get our visas for India, but we were grateful that at least we had our passports. We would somehow have to get our visas while in Bhutan—or else we wouldn't get into India.

The Shit Shovel

UNLIKE THE OTHER COUNTRIES WE'RE VISITING, WE HAVE had to book an organized trip to go to Bhutan. Part of our fifteen-day tour there is a trek in the foothills of the Himalayas that has us camping overnight. Before we leave Bangkok, Ira and I sit in our hotel room to review the two-page list provided by the tour company of items we need to bring. The list includes a flashlight, sleeping bag, and aspirin. We discuss the list and our different interpretations of what is "required" versus what is "optional."

"Is a whisk broom to brush out the dirt from your tent really a required item?" I ask Ira.

Ira agrees that this might be an optional item.

As we're scanning through the list, I say about one item, "I've got to believe that we can rent or buy that in Bhutan."

We continue to read through the list and the "I've got to believe" comment keeps coming for many of the items that seem to me are definitely optional. We laugh about this as we both have no clue what we really need and do not.

We decide that we should get the items we both agree are required: sleeping bags, rain gear, and a shovel for digging a hole after you have done your "business." We locate a five-story shopping center in Bangkok and begin looking for the items. We search for a camping store but all we primarily see are clothing and jewelry stores. There is no directory so there is no way to make sense of the five floors and what goods are sold where.

Ira decides to ask a security guard in broken Thai, "Camping store?"

The security guard nods, indicates he knows what we're looking for, and we follow him. From one end of the floor to the other, we walk through a maze of shirt shops and other clothing stores.

Ira looks at me and whispers, "There is no way he could have understood what I said."

But we keep following him. Finally, he stops and extends his arm toward a store at the end of the path. It is, in fact, a camping store! Amazing! We begin to shop.

First are the sleeping bags. We get lightweight ones that will be warm. They do not have rain gear, so we note to find that elsewhere.

Next is the shovel. I use this opportunity to ask Ira again if he truly believes this is "necessary." In reading about Bhutan, we have learned that the country rigorously restricts the number of people it lets in and is extremely rigid in maintaining its eco-environment.

Ira and I have previously camped at Burning Man in the Nevada desert, where the regulations are very strict, requiring that you "leave no trace."

"Maybe the shovel is the Bhutanese government's way to ensure they keep the environment pristine," Ira says.

"I have to believe that it won't be optional. How are they going to patrol whether we have one?" I ask.

"What if we get there and the other trekkers have their shovels, and we are the only ones without one?" Ira asks. "Would you be willing to lend ours to another trekker?"

I sigh. He has a point. "Okay, let's get the shit shovel! Do we need his and hers, or will one be enough?" I ask.

We find the shovels. There are two kinds: a plastic one similar to a beach shovel I had as a kid and a steel one that could become a family heirloom. The steel one has an additional section that gets screwed into the other, elongating the handle, which could be useful if we need to dig a hole to South America from Bhutan.

We have another discussion on this topic. I'm convinced that the plastic one will be all we need. It's also much lighter to carry.

"I think you're right, considering how heavy our backpacks are already," Ira says.

"Good, it's decided," I say.

"However, having camped in the Nevada desert where the ground is so tough that you need practically need construction rebar to make sure your tent won't blow away, I am not convinced that the plastic one won't fall apart after the first usage," Ira says.

I'm less concerned.

Ira gives his last effort. "Have you ever been trekking in Bhutan? Do you know the consistency of the earth there? Because I do not," he says.

That is how we wind up with the industrial strength shovel and the additional three pounds it weighs. Since Ira has won this discussion, he gets to carry the shovel.

And then we go to the Moonshine bar, under a full moon, to have our last drink in Thailand.

Bhutan: Director of Security

THROUGHOUT THE TRIP, IRA HAS BEEN PRETTY OBSESSED with security, which made sense because he traveled with expensive photography equipment. Our daily routine went something like this:

1. "We have reached lockdown status," Ira announced daily to let me know that all of our valuable belongings had been secured with chains and locks. He would lock them up in cabinets, underneath the bed frame, or wherever he felt they could be tethered to be secure.
2. We agreed never to use the word "laptop" in public. Ira assured me that if someone overheard us saying the L-word, it would make us a prime target for a robbery. So we use a code and referred to it simply as "LT."

Sitting at the designated meeting spot outside the Paro airport, we look around for the other people arriving for our tour. There is only one other woman and us. Then our guide tells us that this is the whole tour.

"Hi, I'm Peggy," the woman says.

"Hi, I'm Joanne and this is my boyfriend Ira," I reply.

"Peggy, did you get all of the items on the list?" Ira asks.

"What list?" Peggy responds.

"What do you mean by 'what list'?" Ira says.

"Just what I said, Ira, 'what list'?"

"The list of required items that we need for our trek."

"Where did this list come from?"

"From our tour operator. Didn't you get the big blue packet?"

"I did get the big blue packet, but it seemed like a bunch of silly articles. I left it home in New York."

"True, there was some non-required reading, however, there were two important pages of items that we HAD to bring."

"Two pages? Well, they are probably used to people coming without the items and should be able to get us whatever we missed."

"Don't be too sure, Peggy. It said right at the top of the page: REQUIRED!"

"So, what was on this list?"

"Very important items such as sleeping bag, flashlight, whisk broom, shovel."

"Whisk broom? Shovel? Why are THEY required?"

"So we can sweep the dust out of our tent. And the shovel to clean up after ourselves. Maybe there are some special restrictions in the Himalayan mountains that we are not aware of, Peggy. I don't want to get fined or thrown out by the Bhutanese if we don't follow their rules."

"I have trekked several times through Tibet and Nepal and was never asked to bring a whisk broom. I think this list of required items was not completely necessary. And as far as the shovel, I am sure that we will make do without it."

I couldn't believe that I was listening to this conversation and feeling grateful that someone else besides me got to witness this craziness. Someone else gets to be a part of the my world. As I sip my butter tea, I realize that Peggy and I are going to get along just fine.

We learn more about Peggy. She explains that she spent twenty years climbing up the corporate ladder and had a successful career as a an advertising agency vice president. She owns a dream apartment in

Chelsea and a house in up-state New York that is used as a weekend getaway. Although she had all the "trappings" of a successful life, she felt that there was something more out there for her. She found respite in meditation and took meditation workshops in New York City. Although these helped, she knew that she had to take her search out of New York. She decided to give it all up and take a trip around the world to get closer to her spirituality. While volunteering in third-world countries, she quickly recognized that the world was a better place once she left the demands of a stress-filled office.

One of her trips was to the hillside town of Dharamsala, India, the adopted home of the Dalai Lama. She studied the teaching of Buddha and her goal was to incorporate these teachings into her life. She meditated on the mountains and decided that she would continue on this path and go to Bhutan.

She chose Bhutan because of its peacefulness, its remoteness, and the lack of stress. She hoped to meet like-minded individuals while on the tour.

Several days later, on the rhodo-dendron trek, we see zero rhododen-drons only tons of mud. When we had booked this tour, we were told that "springtime would be in full bloom and flowers would be spotting up around us." However, due to some weather changes and road construction, our path is completely covered in mud up to our ankles without a flower to be seen anywhere.

Peggy and Joanne on a bridge (Bhutan).
Photo credit: Ira L. Black

We trek alongside yaks, donkeys, and mules and spend half the time navigating past their shit. "I guess those yaks must have been exempt from carrying shovels," Peggy says.

After trekking for eight hours, with sore feet, we finally get to our overnight campsite. Peggy sees Ira with his LT "leash," chains, and locks.

"What are you doing with all that stuff?" she asks.

"I am getting us into lockdown' status," he replies.

"Lockdown status?"

"I need to make sure that nothing happens to the equipment."

"What do you need that for? We are miles away from anyone."

"I would feel more comfortable knowing that they were safe."

"But this is Bhutan. Mostly everyone here is a Buddhist."

"Right, and why should that matter?"

"They believe that if they steal, it will affect their karmic debt. If they steal, they could be reincarnated into a lower life form, like a fly."

"I get all that karma stuff, but I still don't want to take any chances."

Peggy looks at me to see if I can help her make sense out of this.

"Is this how he always is?"

I shrug and say, "He is a little security obsessed."

Later, we discover that Peggy had been in the same Thailand mall that we'd been in—and at the same time. Was she "preparing" for her trip to Bhutan? Was she frantically scouring every corner to get every last item on the list? It turns out that while we were "discussing" which items were necessary versus those that were subject to interpretation, Peggy was comfortably watching *Star Wars: Revenge of the Sith*.

Given we are pretty convinced that we will not need the shovel for the rest of the trip, we decide to donate it to our guide for his future use. Our guide is somewhat shocked and confused when we present it to him. He looks it over and believes it is really well made, whatever it is. He is not really sure what to say, but thanks us just the same. Then we tell him the story of our high-grade shit shovel starting from the hotel discussion in Thailand. Soon, we are all laughing.

Bhutan: Fertility Tour 1

APRIL 2005

IN BHUTAN, YAKS ROAM FREE, AND EVERYONE WEARS THE national uniform of a long skirt, even for men, day and night. This Buddhist country is led by a king who has three wives. Oh, and they are sisters. The traditional dress of the Bhutanese women covers them to their ankles, and they never show affection in public. Given how modest the Bhutanese people are, we are shocked to see that they protect their homes against evil spirits and encourage fertility by hanging flying phalluses on the outside doors of their homes.

One of our tour stops is a temple of the Divine Madman, the fertility god Lam Drukpa Kunley. Chencho, our guide, leads our trio into the temple.

The interior of this holy place is covered with intricate paintings and statues of the Divine Madman, along with hundreds of model phalluses. While we know that this is an important part of Bhutanese culture, we cannot stop giggling.

"Why do you laugh in a temple?" Chencho says, his tone annoyed. "Lam Drukpa Kunley is a Buddhist saint credited with the successful conception of many women. They have traveled from all over the world to pray for pregnancy at his temple. This is no joke."

We drop our heads like scolded children while trying to stifle our laughter.

"Who wants to take part in the fertility ritual?" Chencho asks.

We look at each other and shrug our shoulders. Luckily, Peggy speaks first. "Chencho, I do not want to insult the Divine Madman, but I am coming up on my fiftieth birthday and do not want to have children at this age. I'm going to pass."

"Very well," Chencho replies, his annoyance growing. "And what about you two? Are you going to tell me that you do not want children either?"

"We do want children, but not now. We are on this trip, you see, and...," I begin.

Chencho cuts me off mid-sentence. "He will know when you are ready. Come, follow me."

Ira and I look at each other. Even though he doesn't say a word, I know what he's thinking, "How do you get us mixed up in this stuff, Joanne?"

Ira and I kneel before Chencho as instructed. It is a feast for the eyes, with so much color that my eyes didn't know where to rest. Reaching into a brightly painted, ornate cabinet, Chencho pulls out the Sacred Phallus, modeled after the Divine Madman's. It's made of wood painted in reds and yellows. I'm impressed by how ornate it is. Chencho waves it over our heads, yelling prayers loud enough for even old Drukpa Kunley to hear. I dare not look at Ira for fear of exploding with laughter. But I do sneak a peek at Peggy. She looks quietly amused.

India: Arriving

WE FLY OUT OF THE BHUTAN'S PARO AIRPORT, WHICH required us to walk on the tarmac to board our flight and head to Kolkata, India, which is in the East-most corner next to Bangladesh. Luckily we were able to get our Indian visa in Bhutan. It is only for a month but we don't need that long. Going to get in and get out.

I am thinking about the last thing that Peggy said to me, "Take a video of Ira once you get out of the airport and onto the street. I want to see his reaction." I'm not sure exactly why she said this, but I can imagine it's going to be funny.

After we land and get our bags, we head toward the streets to get a ride to our hotel. We planned where we would stay the first two nights so that we wouldn't have to look for a place when we landed.

The minute we set foot outside the airport, are hit hard: The heat. The sounds. The smells. The traffic. The air quality.

So very different from the cool mountain air of Bhutan's Himalayan soaring mountains.

"Need a ride?" a tuk-tuk driver yells to Ira. The tuk tuk reminds me of a tricked-out golf cart.

"No. We're good," Ira replies.

"Mister. Mister. Tuk-tuk ride?"

"Over here, sir."

"Hello! Mister! Best tuk-tuk!"

Tuk-tuk drivers abound and they all want to drive the foreigners—us—to our destination.

We see a taxi and opt for it to get us to our hotel. Once we settle inside the taxi, the chaos of the airport still all around us, I whip out my camera and turn it to video mode.

Pointing the camera at Ira, I ask, "Ira, you just landed in India. How do you feel?"

"I feel like I just got ripped off," he says.

India: Fertility Tour 2

I READ ABOUT THE POWERFUL FEMALE HINDU GODDESS, Kali. In pictures, she looks darkly evil. Sometimes she holds aloft the severed heads of men she has conquered, but, apparently, this representation is in the name of fighting evil to promote goodness. I can never resist the lure of powerful women, so I suggest to Ira that we go to Kali's temple.

It's May. At home, flowers would be bursting into bloom, cool mornings would transition into comfortable days. In India, it's worse than August in New York City. Streets shimmer with sweltering heat. Street vendors trying to sell us marigolds, prayer beads, and cakes as offerings to the goddess surround us. My mother taught me never to go empty-handed when visiting, so I pick up a necklace made of bright yellow marigolds.

Although the temple was only 200 years old, it looks as if it has stood here much longer. Visiting Indians carry goats with them to slaughter as offerings to Kali. We join a line of people that stretches all the way around the temple. A man wearing a long white robe of a Brahmin monk approaches us. He's holding what appears to be a holy book. It's thick and dusty with a satin page marker.

"Do you want to take a special tour?" We have read warnings that we should be wary of people posing as Brahmin monks to get a donation, so we are somewhat skeptical.

"No," says Ira. "We're fine. We don't need a tour."

"You will give the temple a small donation and I will not only take you on a special tour, but I will also perform a special ceremony for you." He is not going to let us off so easily.

"We don't want a special ceremony," I say. "We're just here to see Kali."

"I can get you past that long line," the Brahmin says.

Ira looks at me. I'm beginning to wilt in the heat as quickly as the marigolds I'm carrying. "Let's try," Ira says.

In seconds we are whisked past the line to confront a statue of the goddess Kali. She's fierce looking, all in black, her eyes a furious red. The Brahmin brings us to an altar covered with candles, incense, flowers, and offerings to the Goddess. I add the necklace.

In a cloud of incense smoke, he invokes her spirit and says prayers in Hindu. Then he ties a red ritual string to each of our wrists and tells us, "If this string stays on for seven days, it means that the ritual was a success."

"And what was the ritual for?" I ask. "Good luck?"

"No, it was a fertility ritual."

"Oh," Ira says. He looks at me with that already familiar expression, which means, "What have you gotten us into now, Joanne?"

Seven days later, the string bracelets are still on. We hope that Kali is smart enough to realize that we do not want the fertility to kick in while we are still on our trip.

All these unplanned fertility rituals have me thinking about another fertility tour. My first encounter with the world of fertility worship was with my friend Allison on a small island in Mexico. The Spanish who arrived there in the sixteenth century named it Isla Mujeres, meaning "Island of Women" because of the many cult images of the moon goddess, Ixchel. We rented a golf cart for transportation and were on our way to an area known for its historic lighthouse. Along the way we noticed a sanctuary dedicated to Ixchel, "mistress of all paths to fertility." Since the sixteenth century, she was known as "the goddess of making children." In 1988, Hurricane Gilbert hit the island and the sanctuary is now mostly a pile of rocks.

At that time, two of my close friends had been trying to get pregnant for years and were having a difficult time. I thought, "Why not say a prayer for them? It couldn't hurt." While praying for Ixchel to grant babies to two wonderful women, I added an extra request for me. "Oh, Ixchel, and while you are at it, one day when I want to get pregnant, maybe you can remember me. Not now, but one day."

And that was that, or almost. I did add another message to be safe: "Don't confuse me with my friends. Them, now—me later."

India: Birthdays—Buddha's and Mine

MAY 2005

WHILE CELEBRATING THE BUDDHA'S BIRTHDAY IN Darjeeling, Ira asks me where I want to spend my birthday. I am torn between a few places that I want to see in India. Dharamsala? Varanasi? Rajasthan?

Over the ensuing days, he asks me again and again. He's pretty insistent that we pick an amazing spot. With so many great places to choose from, this feels like a big decision. I think it would be cool to be in Rajasthan. Brightly colored saris against the Golden City. Camel safaris. Ornate temples. "Are you sure that's where you want to be?" he asks a few times.

"Yeah, what's the big deal? It's just my birthday." And then it hits me. Ira is asking because he wants to be somewhere special in the world —to ask me to marry him! And it's our anniversary weekend too! Double success!

That's why he keeps asking. That's why he wants to be sure it's the perfect place. What better place to ask than on a camel safari?

I'm thinking that a life shared is actually a good thing. I will act surprised when he asks me. I won't admit to him that I knew he planned it all along.

India: Lychees

MAY 2005

WERE WE JUST POISONED? IRA AND I LOOK AT EACH OTHER with frightened looks in our eyes. This might be the end. Our parents kept asking if we were still in India. Maybe we would be here forever.

Ira and I are on an overnight train, traveling through the Rajasthani desert on our way to Jaisalmer. We have assigned seats but are packed in. People and bags are helter skelter. The scent of jasmine, curry, and sweat fills the air. If we would have been in the United States, this train would have been retired many decades ago.

There's a lovely multigenerational Indian family sitting across from us, the women wearing saris in a patchwork of color that brightened up the drab seats. The grandmother reaches over to hand us a Lychee from her bag of snacks, we accept it. The gold bangles on her arms jingle with a sweet sound. The sweet sticky fruit is divine, its juice running down our arms.

I remember what a waiter in Darjeeling said, "Do not take any food from strangers. It's known that tourists are poisoned on the train and found the next morning with passports and wallets stolen," he said. "Or never found at all."

But we whisper to each other, "It's a piece of fruit that is covered by a natural hard shell; it can't be tampered with."

"But maybe they injected it with poison by using a syringe," Ira says. "It's a great decoy meant to make us feel safe."

And the family seemed so kind. Was it possible that they were really this nice? We wait to see when the poison will kick in.

I GREW UP IN THE TOUGH STREETS OF JERSEY CITY, NEW Jersey. It was at a time that all of the families we knew were trying to escape. Our house was broken into several times. I'd walk from my car at night with my keys wedged between my fingers in case I was attacked so I could fight back.

But my brothers and I loved living there growing up. One time, when our parents said they were thinking of moving out as well, we protested. "But all of our friends are here. We don't want to move to the suburbs" It was a thought worse than death. Boredom. We had family who lived in the suburbs. And it seemed so *bor-ring* to us.

As a result, trust was something we had to learn. To not look over our shoulders all the time, waiting for someone to try to rob us.

India: Naan Proposal

Since the primary adventure thing to do in the desert is a camel safari, wherever you walk or go, someone from somewhere will ask, "Mister, camel safari? Camel safari, Mister?" They always address the man, as if a woman can't possibly make a decision about going on a camel safari.

"So, babe, are we going to do that camel safari that we talked about?" I ask Ira.

"The Jews spent forty years trying to get out of the desert, and now you want us to go back in?" he says.

"Ha, very funny, And, yes, I do want to go in." Ira knows I am Catholic, and we don't have the same relationship with the desert as the tribes of Israel do. I do realize that it is really hot. Like cooking-up-a-naan-on-the-sidewalk hot.

"I'm definitely not sure being on a camel in the desert in the hottest month in India is a good idea," Ira says.

Is he just trying to throw me off the scent of the impending proposal?

Just then, like something out of a movie, someone on the street yells over to us, "Mister, mister, camel safari? Camel safari, mister?"

"I think it was meant to be," I say. "Babe, you and me riding camels; it will be great." Just our luck, as it turns out, our hotel offers camel safaris. However, they advise us that due to the debilitating heat, they would recommend that instead of the typical three to four-day trek, we only do an overnight safari.

"Joanne, these guys do this for a living, and they are saying that given the heat, they would only go out for an overnight. Maybe we should wait until we are in India at a cooler time."

But I don't seem to be catching the clue Ira is trying to send my way.

I reply, "We can do an overnight, right? You and me, sleeping in the desert? How bad can it be?"

We discover that there are two kinds of safaris: a touristy one and a non-touristic version. We decide to opt for the non-touristic one, where we are guaranteed that it will not be overrun with those pesky tourists.

The next day we are set for our camel adventure. Although we opted for the non-touristic tour, we personify tourist by buying camel safari attire. We're told that turbans are supposed to keep us cool. We're also told it's what the local desert people wear. So we buy turbans. We also buy very light white camel safari outfits. We are ready.

We meet our guide in the hotel lobby at three in the afternoon. We head out by jeep for about an hour through the desert. Wind- and sand-dusted and a little queasy, we arrive at a checkpoint where we find three camels waiting for us: one for me, one for Ira, and one which will be shared by our two guides.

Ira asks me the question that has by now become a running joke between us during the trip, "Whose idea was this?"

Only I am not sure it is really a joke for Ira anymore.

We start to get on the camels. They look just like camels I've seen in pictures: large, dusty, but overall friendly. There is a scent of dirt in the air.

Just as we are positioned on them, they bolt upright like a rocket being launched. Imagine trying to keep hold of a missile as it rockets upward. That is how hard it is to gain my balance when the camel rises. I let out a loud, "Ahhh!"

Ira lets out a "Whoo!"

Our confidence increases the more time we spend getting on our camels, and we set off into the desert in the early evening. It's still sweltering. Our turbans are not effective at keeping us cool and comfortable as was advertised, but then again it is 118 degrees, we are in the desert, and there are no trees for shade. Ira makes sure that we both drink lots of water during our ride.

Riding the camels turns out to be quite fun. I'm taking pictures and videos of us, the camels, and our guides from my high viewpoint. After about three hours of riding, we reach the spot for dinner and camping. Our guides cook dinner for us over a bonfire, which consists of spicy meat, dal, mixed vegetables, rice, and a baati churma which is a hard unleavened bread famous in that region. Our meal is completed with chai. Life seems as if it can't get any better as we settle in to watch the sunset.

"Aren't you glad we did this?" I ask.

"Yes, I think you were right when you said it was going to be a fun experience."

I wonder if this is the moment when he's going to pop the question. I mean, how much better can it get than this? Camel safari. On a blanket. Sunset. What a story we will get to tell our parents! *Where did he hide the ring? Maybe it's in his turban.*

As we're enjoying our meal, I hear scuttling in the sand near where we're sitting. We realize these are desert beetles—and not your ordinary, run-of-the-mill beetles. They are equal in size to our Nokia flip phones. They are like menacing scarabs, thick-shelled and impenetrable, like they can survive a nuclear war and evolve being stronger and faster. They seem to swarm up from the bowels of the earth, head straight toward us, and surround our blanket.

Then the unthinkable happens: One by one, they scuttle *onto* the blanket. We're not sure what's attracting them, the food, the water, or us.

They seem to find me especially attractive. Unfortunately for them, I don't return their fondness. I'm pretty upset that our romantic dinner in the desert under the stars is being ruined by these cell phones with legs. I'm not sure what to do with this emotion. Our guides tell us that they do not bite and will not harm us in any way.

I don't really care about what they can or cannot do to us, I'm pretty freaked out. The silence of the desert is pierced with the sounds of me shouting

I know my mom thought Ira would protect me from the wind. I imagine she never thought he'd have to protect me from the desert beetles.

Ira and the guides do their best to keep the offensive beasts away from me so we can try to get back to our dinner, but there are too many of them and they are everywhere we want to be. And now it's dark and we're not able to find them.

One decides that my lap is a nice place to spend some time. When I realize this, I am sure the scream can be heard back in Delhi. Dinner is definitely over, and we quickly head to our tent for the night.

Things don't get any easier over in the tent area. Ira spends about twenty minutes trying to make sure that no beetles have crawled into our sleeping bags or somewhere else in the tent.

"Are you sure you got them all?"

"Yes," Ira says. But I can tell from his face that he's not exactly sure.

Plus, our tent has become a sauna. We open the small flap at the top of the tent and believe that we will get some air circulating as there seems to be a breeze of hot air blowing. But our luck from the beetles seems to be extending to our tent experience. We are only able to open the zipper of the first tent door, so there is a mesh between us and the other flying bugs. The mesh is great at keeping out the bugs, but it has the added bonus of also keeping out any breeze that might help to cool us down.

We have laid our sleeping bags on the floor for additional cushioning. We try to get comfortable, but the desert beetles have gotten into our thoughts, and we're bugged out.

In the steam room that is our tent, we have two choices: wear as few clothes as possible to enable us to be somewhat cooler or leave our clothes on as a buffer against the beetles and other critters of the night.

"Are you wearing your socks? I don't think I've ever seen you sleep with socks," I ask.

Ira responds somewhat reluctantly, "Yes."

I think he doesn't want to tell me he's afraid of the beetles too. I wonder if he's gotten all of them from the tent. We lie awake unable to enjoy the stars just outside the tent. We swat at the flies and other things that we imagine are crawling on us. We try to sleep with our eyes and mouths shut.

"Whose idea was this anyway?" Ira asks in an effort to try to eek out some humor in this situation. It is really not funny.

"Maybe if we position ourselves facing the other direction of the tent, it might be cooler," I say. I try it out. "It's much better over here."

Ira moves to get into position but the tent on that side is slanted and narrower from top to bottom. Since he is taller than me, he's struggling to position his head at the edge of the tent.

"I'm imagining I am cooler," Ira says.

"Is it working?" I ask.

"Unfortunately, I don't feel cooler. I feel just as hot. And now more claustrophobic."

"You better move back to the other side then."

On the other side, however, there is one more element that we have to endure. It seems that while the breeze cannot penetrate the mesh opening of the tent, the sand is fine enough to make it through. So, in addition to the unbearable heat, the thought of overgrown desert beetles crawling on us, and other flying insects buzzing around us, there is also a slight but steady mist of sand that is being dumped on our faces. We're now past the point of miserable to a new state that we don't even believe has a name.

We find ourselves wishing for the air-assisted room in the Desert Haveli.

"Are you okay?" Ira asks me.

"Yeah." I try to stay calm. And breathe the hot air without taking in too much sand. I guess this was not the most romantic place in the world for Ira to ask me to marry him.

Somehow, we make it through the night. And wake up with the sun. We're sweaty, grossed out and exhausted from barely sleeping. I'd say miserable.

Ira looks pretty rough. Sweat pouring down. Hair Einstein-esqe. I imagine I look the same.

"We made it," I say with a smile.

Ira grunts.

I get out of our tent to see the expanse of the desert. There's nothing else on the horizon. Just sand and hills and more sand. Our guides have already packed up and are sitting waiting for us to have the breakfast they made for us which was a thick chapati coated with caramelized sugar.

"Coffee?"

"Yes, please."

As he brings me coffee, I say, "Hot in the tent last night, right?"

"We slept outside. No tent for us," he replies.

"No tent?"

"No, no tent."

"Weren't you afraid of the desert beetles crawling on you in the middle of the night?"

"They don't bite. We're not scared."

I imagine it was much cooler sleeping outside with no sand mist falling on their faces. But still. The thought of the beetles crawling on them freaks me out a bit.

Ira comes out of the tent and joins me for our morning breakfast.

We get back on our steadfast camels, which we've named Charlie and Rocket, and ride back through the desert. I wonder if Ira was going to ask me to marry him but chose not to because of the "situation." Or did he not even plan to ask me in the desert? Or on this trip? Was I picking up the wrong signals?

AFTER RIDING AND RIDING OUR CAMELS FOR HOURS, WE get to the town with our Jeep. We're happy to see a moving object that is not a camel. We pile into the Jeep and take a long deep breath of hot air.

"That was a tough night, huh?" I say to Ira.

"Yeah, well maybe even tougher for me," he replies.

"Why's that? Were you as scared of the beetles as me?" I reply.

"Nah. You won on that one," he says.

"I didn't think it was a competition."

"Well, I thought I was going into shock," he replies.

"What? Shock? Why didn't you tell me?" I ask.

"I didn't want to upset you," he says.

"I think if you went into shock and I found you dead in the tent, that would've upset me!" I say.

"Yeah, but here's what I was thinking," he says. "How long did we ride the camels?"

"About three hours."

"Right. And how long was the Jeep ride?"

"I guess about an hour."

"Right. We were at least four hours from civilization. It would have been too tough to get any help."

"So it would've been better for me to wake up with you dead in the tent?" I ask. "What were your symptoms?"

"My breathing was short, my heart was racing fast, and I felt like I was slipping into a new dimension," he says. "I generally was not in a good situation."

"That doesn't sound good."

"No. At first, I thought if I was destined to go into shock, it was obviously meant for me to not be able to get help. If God wanted me to get help, why would he or she have chosen such a remote place for my first experience of shock? There was nothing more to do but accept the wave of shock. I was tired of the sand, the beetles, the tent, and especially the heat. I lay awake completely still, waiting for the shock to hit me."

"That sounds awful," I say. "I'm really shocked you didn't tell me. Pun intended. So what happened next?"

"I decided that I was not going to go out like that, not this way, not in this non-touristic camel safari ride in the desert. I would've eaten a desert beetle if they told me it was an ancient tribal healing medicine. I decided that living was my fate," he says.

"I'm glad you lived. I love you, babe. Next time you think you are going into shock, please tell me," I say.

I guess the desert was not the most romantic place in the world for Ira to ask me to marry him.

India: Blue Envelope

IRA AND I ARE TRAVELING THROUGH THE RAJASTHANI desert, an off-the-beaten-track vacation mecca in India. Men wear multi-colored turbans, the women in bright saris. The landscape is desert with towering ancient fortresses

During our stay, we encounter exceptionally friendly Indian men who work at guesthouses and restaurants. Inevitably, after three minutes of conversation, each will flash a picture in front of Ira and me, showing each one with their respective "girlfriends." The girl-friends always seem to be Paris Hilton look-alikes, who live in other parts of the developed world.

Having just come from Thailand, where we couldn't help but notice many stunningly beautiful young Thai women arm-in-arm with their George Costanza-like "boyfriends," we began to sense a pattern, which is exactly the opposite here in Rajasthan. Here the young tourism-men earn the monthly equivalent of what their "girlfriends" spend on one handbag. Yet, the pictures show each couple smiling together.

I'm not sure if these women know that they have "a boyfriend in India" or if they have merely enjoyed a Lawrence of Arabia-type fling while passing through.

Another possibility is that these women simply took an innocent tourist picture with a friendly man. Now this man presents it as a photo of his girlfriend to anyone who takes the time to look. I realize that I, too, have taken several photographs with friendly Indian men. I feel a knot inside my stomach. How are they being represented to others?

We stay a month in Rajasthan and befriend the people who work at our Haveli, which is a former palace like most Havelis in India are. To help fund the upkeep of the palaces, they rent out rooms to tourists. For approximately twelve US dollars per day, one could stay in a palace and act like a princess. Okay, so not really a princess but a very important person.

One day when I go to the lobby, I see one of these new friends, Samsingh, and mention to him that after leaving India, I'll be going to Russia. He looks surprised and tells me that his "girlfriend" lives there. This is my opportunity to find out more about the "girlfriend" pattern. I ask some detailed questions. "What is her name? How did you meet? When did you see her last? When will you see her again?"

Samsingh's tale is similar to the other stories I have heard from the men with the pictures: his girlfriend, Natasha, had traveled through the Rajasthani desert on vacation. They met, fell in love, took a camel safari, and enjoyed two romantic weeks together. He says he loves Natasha very much and hopes to marry her one day.

Having learned English by working with tourists, Samsingh speaks the language well but cannot read or write it. He tells me he is having difficulty reaching Natasha via phone. He asks if I can help him write a love letter to her. He seems sincere. I feel that there is a chance for me to help him contact her, not to mention that I can learn more about this situation. I agree to write the letter. He tells me to meet him in the lobby at four that afternoon because he has to go out and buy something.

My mission had originally been to get Ira and me chai tea in the lobby. I return to our room and find Ira waiting.

"Everything okay?" he asks.

"Yeah, well, sort of, but I kinda got myself involved in helping someone out," I reply.

"Who are you helping out now?" he asks.

I fill him in on my writing date.

"How do you get yourself involved in these things?" he asks.

"He loves her but can't write the letter himself. How could I say 'no'?"

"Easy! You just say 'no'," Ira says with a smile.

We laugh knowing that's not possible for me.

At 4:00 p.m. Samsingh is eagerly waiting, smiling from ear to ear. He pulls out a big blue envelope and extends his hand to me. Inside the envelope is a card with a blond-haired, blue-eyed couple hugging on the front. When I open the card, a dozen red hearts pop out. It reminds me of cards I used to get and give in high school.

"Do you think she will like it?" he asks.

"How could she not?" I respond, knowing he probably spent half his weekly salary on it.

He is proud of his card. I sit down with my pen, waiting to take down his words.

He starts with, "How come you never call me anymore?" Not the best way to start a love letter, I think to myself. I advise him that we should discuss and take notes before writing in the card.

"Do you have a nickname for Natasha?" I ask.

"Yes, I call her 'dovey'," he replies.

"Great. Let's start with that. Do you miss her?"

"Oh yes, very much."

"What if we tell her, 'I miss you and think of you every day'?"

"Yes, yes, that is good!"

"So do you want to see her soon?"

"Yes, please, as soon as she can return to India."

"What if we tell her, 'I think about how nice it will be to see you again'?"

"Oh yes, write that."

And so it goes for close to two hours.

He's very happy with the final product. I am, too. With a feeling of accomplishment, I hand him the letter. He looks at me strangely and says, "I thought that since you were going to Moscow that you could just take it to her."

I remember my earlier conversation with Ira and think, "How do I get myself involved in these things?"

"Well, Moscow is a big place, and I am not sure if I will be anywhere near where she is," I say.

"But the mail system is really bad in India and there is a good chance that it will never reach her if I mail it from here," he persists.

I try again. "Yes, true, but how can I possibly locate her? Russia is a big country."

"Not to worry. I will give you a way to find her."

After all this, I feel like I have to finish what I started. Damn! Reluctantly I take the letter. *What have I gotten myself into now? Wait until Ira hears this!*

Following our travel itinerary, Ira and I continue through India with the Blue Envelope in my backpack. It joins us at the holy lake in Pushkar as well as the Taj Mahal.

Writing Samsingh's love letter got me to reflect on my own love story. I realize that having someone to share the experience with is something I love. I also realize that having someone to care for me, who respects me and my strong will, does not take away my freedom.

Joanne with the blue envelope in front of the metro (Moscow, Russia). Photo credit: Ira L. Black

I'm also thinking about all the random couples along the way who are shocked that Ira and I have spent so much time together and still can stand being near each other. "I'm on a one-week vacation and I'm sick of my spouse already," these couples say.

But we are not sick of each other. We will sometimes cram together in a single-sized bed because we're staying in budget rooms with bunk beds—and being in our own separate beds seems too far away from each other.

India: Spice Girl

MAY 2005

I READ ABOUT MV SPICES IN THE *Lonely Planet* GUIDEBOOK. Mohanlal Verhomal, the owner of MV Spices is a legend in Jodhpur's Clock Tower Market. Jodhpur is in Rajasthan, which is the westernmost part of India. We search the shop out and find it.

Then we learn that Mohanlal Verhomal has passed away. I spend time talking with his daughter Usha, who is keeping the business going with her sisters.

"Running a spice store within the spice markets of Jodhpur is not a place for a young woman," Usha Verhomal's father used to tell her and her five sisters. Covered in her pink sari, Usha sits on a bench so small that it looks like it was made for children. We are huddled inside a small spice shop away from the deafening din of the market. She pours saffron tea. Its bright burnt orange scent and earthy flavor is like no other that I've ever had. I'm surrounded by spices of exhilarating colors, which are stored on row after row of shelves. With a mixture of scents combining the mixtures of spices. Scents of cardamom, cloves, and cumin swirl through the air. Spice shelves stacked from floor to ceiling explode in bright yellows, oranges, and reds.

"My father died suddenly last year," she says. "He kept trying to have a son to one day take over the business, without success. I am the oldest of his six daughters. Since there is no one else to support us, I have taken over the running of his business." She is poised.

"Had you worked with your father here in the store before taking over the business?" I ask.

"No, since he did not think that the market was a proper place for a woman, I was not here in the shop with him. I had to learn his business from notes that he left over the years," She says. Usha describes how difficult a time she is having running this business that she only recently inherited. The business suffers in part because people that her father had long-standing relationships with do not want to do business with a woman.

She describes with great pride the demeanor and charisma her father had with others. She seems convinced that she does not have all of her father's talents, but that she has his strength and is doing what she can to make him proud. Someone needs to run the shop and support the rest of the family or else they will have nothing.

MV Spice wannabes surround Usha's shop. There are shops next to hers with similar sounding names: MU Spices, MW Spices. We even hear shouts of "our spices are better than MV's" as we pass by. MV is the only spice shop in Jodhpur that is continually recommended by the *Lonely Planet* guidebook, even though many of the others have signs saying that *they* are recommended by *Lonely Planet*.

"Are there any other women in the market that you can get together with to develop a support group and discuss the challenges of being a female business owner?"

She replies that there is another woman in the market who had taken over her husband's business after he died. "I have tried to approach her before, and she did not seem to be interested in developing a relationship with me." Usha believes that the other woman thought that helping her would be at the other woman's detriment.

"Are there any woman-run organizations outside the market that can assist you in your business?" I ask, determined to find a way to help her.

"In Mumbai, there are many women doing very progressive things, but here in Jodhpur, things are still very traditional."

But then, somewhere between the first and second cup of tea, there seems to be a shift in Usha.

Although she has indicated that she had tried some of these efforts in the past, an openness is building in her. She begins to ask questions. "Maybe this is not Mumbai, but why couldn't I help to bring more forward-thinking ideas to Jodhpur? Why can't I start a group to bring other women that are having a similar struggle together to bring about change?"

Usha is determined to continue in her father's path and keep the shop. She is expanding the Internet business and is shipping to customers all over the world. With her online policy of "pay only *after* you receive the merchandise," customers trust that the products will arrive at their door safely.

MV Spices not only sells spices, teas, and curry mixes, they are also known for some of their special blends. One of these is the "Winter Tonic," which is described as "a herbal mix of spices. It's good for warming up your body, bad sneeze, cough, and sexual strength." Another special blend is the "Brain Food," which is said to get your brainpower working overtime.

A picture of her father, surrounded by flowers, is displayed above the shop office. I think her father would be proud that she is trying to do things in her own way.

India: Pushkar's Holy Lake

JUNE 2005

A CITY ON A LAKE. A HOLY LAKE. A LAKE SO HOLY THAT IT IS scattered with churches and temples and mosques. Jains. Muslims. Buddhists. Sikhs. Christians. All in close proximity. All living in harmony. I can't help but imagine that if the world was more like Pushkar, it would be a much better place.

I'm sitting on the stairs overlooking the lake.

There's so much to watch. People having funeral ceremonies. People doing the everyday things they do here. Bathing. Washing their clothes. Birds are flying and are part of the scene.

I think about my brother Robert. I have this sensation that he is here with me. I know that in the normal world, he cannot be. Maybe in this altered state of this holy lake he can be.

When I was twelve, he was eighteen. Robert was a super-talented musician, gymnast, and an awesome big brother. He was always looking out for me and teaching me life lessons. He treated me like a person and not just his little sister. There was one time where I was learning to play guitar but didn't want to practice. He drew a cartoon of how much stronger we get when we practice.

He had fallen in love with a girl. She left him. And broke his heart. He used drugs to ease the pain. The drugs were too powerful for him.

He became a different person. More distant. Not his wonderful self. A person I couldn't recognize. I wanted so desperately for the "old" Robert to come back. He had to come back. I needed him.

He was my protector.

But he didn't come back. He went further and further away from me. From himself. There were moments when we thought he had a chance. But the drugs were too powerful. And he lost his life to them.

And I was crushed. And hurt. How could he do this to me? To my parents? My mom experienced the pain that no mom should feel. The death of her son.

Now I feel him with me in this moment on the stairs.

And then I remember the date. June 10th. Robert's birthday.

I know that he is a guiding light and continues to look out for me.

India: Next Stop The Taj Mahal

JUNE 2005

ON A BUS RIDE TO THE TAJ MAHAL, I LET IRA KNOW THAT I thought he was going to propose to me on my birthday. I share my disappointment and question whether he wants to share his life with me.

I'm in the aisle seat.

Ira's in the window seat, trapped. Ira tries to give a possible reason for the lack of seizing the moment.

I made the leap of faith to want to be with him and he is not jumping with me. The bus is not moving because the driver had to make an unscheduled stop which left us just sitting there for thirty minutes. When the bus driver returns, Ira can't take the pressure and freaks out on the bus driver.

We are heading to a shrine dedicated to the undying love a man had for his wife. Conversely, our relationship is stalled like this bus.

In addition to what is happening, or more accurately not happening in my love life, I think about my dwindling bank account. With every town, country, tour, the balance dips lower and lower.

It isn't that I intentionally choose to become a vegetarian in India, but it just feels like the right thing to do.

One, it's hotter than hot, so sitting down to eat meat doesn't seem appealing.

Two, we're walking alongside cows on the street. Sacred cows. Holy cows! They kind of become our friends. There's a specific cow, who I name Betsy, who I really love, and I think she loves me back. So the thought of eating animals just doesn't seem right.

Three, there are so many amazing things to eat that do not include meat that it really doesn't even feel like a sacrifice.

One day I say to Ira, "Hey, babe, this 'accidental vegetarianism' thing seems to be working for me. I feel pretty energetic. And I weigh less than I've weighed in my entire adult life."

"Really? But you love meat. Do you think it's going to be difficult?" Ira asks.

"The idea of eating meat again is just not feeling good right now. I think I'm going to stick with it."

"Well, let me know how I can support you," Ira says.

"I think it's going to be really easy. I really don't feel like having meat at all," I say.

Ira looks at me with a surprised look. "We'll see how long you can go. And I'll try not to eat bacon in front of you."

Lithuania: Accidental Vegetarian

JUNE 2005

OUR PLAN IS TO HEAD TO RUSSIA AFTER INDIA. Unfortunately, getting our Russian visas before we left the U.S. was impossible because our entry into Russia was too far in the future. But we didn't really think that would be a problem; we would just get our Russian visas in India. That, however, is proving to be a problem. Well, more than a problem. Impossible.

So, we are a bit stuck.

Ira's friend Marius lives in Lithuania. They knew each other when they both lived in Chicago. Ira calls him to see if he can help us in any way in getting the visas.

Ira and Marius trying on hats at an outdoor market (Lithuania). Photo credit: Joanne Flynn Black

"Ira, Ira, come to Lithuania and we will get it worked out for you," Marius says. "No problem."

"Are you sure?" Ira asks.

"Ira, Ira, yes, come stay with me."

We call Aeroflot Airlines and change our tickets to go to Lithuania instead of Russia. And that's how we end up with the funniest and most generous man on the planet. Our flight lands in Vilnius, the capital of Lithuania. We disembark, get our bags, and make our way through the airport crowds.

"Ira! Ira! Over here!" Marius yells when he sees us. They greet each other and immediately hug. Slaps on the back and lots of smiles all around.

"I'd like you to meet Joanne," Ira says.

"Joanne. Joanne. Lovely to meet you," Marius says. "You must be tired from your journey. Let's get you home."

"Ira. Ira. You look good. Strong like bull," Marius says. "It must be from carrying all that camera equipment."

"You look great too," Ira replies.

"Me? Oh, I look like model," Marius says.

"You do look like a model," Ira says.

"Model. Only a Home De-Pot model," he jokes. Saying the pot part just like pot.

We laugh and are whisked away with him in his fast sleek BMW.

We arrive at his home in downtown Vilnius and get settled in. The luxury of having a queen-sized bed in someone's home in a former eastern bloc country does not escape me.

After we have rested and freshened up, Marius says, "Joanne, Joanne, I will take you to an amazing place for dinner."

The amazing place serves a Lithuanian specialty called Cepelinas, also known as Zeppolini. It's like a giant, stuffed calzone the size of a football filled with meat. Its taste is truly amazing like a calzone on steroids.

My meat-eating days are back.

"IRA, IRA, YOU SHOULD GO TO GRUTAS PARKAS," MARIUS says.

"What is that?" Ira asks.

"It's a park of all of the toppled Soviet statues. Like Disneyland. But different. You will go. It will be fun. You will see," Marius says.

That's how we wind up next to larger-than-life-sized statues of Lenin.

We learn that in 1990, when Lithuania regained its independence from Soviet rule, all of the Soviet statues were taken down and dumped in different spots. In 2001, a wealthy farmer-turned-entrepreneur named Viliumus Malinauskas requested access to all of the statues so he could build a privately held museum. Being so close to these statues and understanding the role they played in the history of Lithuania, is truly a powerful experience.

"IRA, IRA, YOU MUST GO TO THE HILL OF CROSSES," MARIUS says.

So, off we go with Yolita, Marius' wife, who is pregnant.

She is wearing a beautiful blue and white dress. The color of the sky.

It is believed that the first crosses were left here in 1831. There are estimated to be 100,000 crosses now.

People bring a cross each time they visit. Marius gives us some crosses to bring so we won't arrive empty-handed.

"The Pope visited here," Yolita says. On September 7, 1993, Pope John Paul II visited, declaring it a place for hope, peace, love, and sacrifice. The place is magical. Crosses everywhere. Big ones, little ones, made of concrete, made out of plastic. Bright colors or plain wood. Every kind of cross you can imagine.

It felt magical, spiritual and surreal all at the same time.

MARIUS OWNS A COFFEE-ROASTING FACILITY, AND WE GO there so that Ira can take some photos to promote the brand.

When we have a break on the photo shoot, Ira says, "Babe, because we made this additional stop in Lithuania, we're going to eat into the time we have planned for Russia. I'm thinking we will need to arrive later in Spain to meet Trevor."

Trevor was our only friend who took us up on the offer to meet somewhere in the world during our trip. And we had a date to meet in Spain already planned.

"I think you need to call Trevor and let him know this," I say.

"I don't think Trevor will mind. It will just be a few days," Ira says.

"Oh, really? I think he will mind. We've planned this for months with him. Why don't you call him and see what he says?"

"I'll call him in a few days."

"You really need to call him now," I say. I know Trevor will put a stop to this madness.

Ira steps out of the coffee roastery and makes a call on his Nokia flip phone.

I watch him from the window. He paces back and forth. He snaps his phone closes and comes inside.

"How did that go?" I ask.

"*Well...*Trevor said, 'Oh, really? You're going to be arriving later in Spain than what we planned? I'll be arriving in Madrid when we planned. You figure out where you'll be on that day.'"

"What should we do?" I ask.

"I think we need to be in Spain the day we said we would," Ira says.

Lithuania: The Rocks

JUNE 2005

IN ADDITION TO THE COUNTLESS PHOTOGRAPHS IRA HAS taken of the amazing people and places we have seen, he starts a new series of fine artwork that involves rocks. On the beach in Klaipeda, we find excellent rocks for this new series.

Marius sees Ira photographing rocks and asks, "I-ra, what are you doing?"

"I'm photographing the balance of movement and static objects, and the rocks bring an exceptional texture to these," Ira replies.

Marius, ever the helpful host, mentions to Ira that his mother has an exquisite collection of rocks that he's sure she would be happy to offer for Ira's new series.

I'm wondering how different the rocks can be compared to the ones we're seeing right here on the beach. Then I guess it is like when we pick up the best seashells we find while at the beach. They've been selected; they're the best of the rocks.

Before Ira can even try to resist his offer, Marius is on his cell phone to his mother. Marius is talking fast in Lithuanian, but we can make out a few words, "Labas, Momma, blah, blah, I-ra, blah blah, photograph blah."

Marius hangs up the phone. "It is set. My mom has agreed to let me use her rocks."

Later that day, we are at Marius' mother's house. It's a charming home, filled with photos, handmade blankets, and genuine warmth. We meet her for the first time, although she has heard a good amount about us. We kiss and hug.

She does not speak much English and our pathetic Lithuanian is useless other than as a show of respect that we are trying to communicate with her. Marius plays translator. She motions for Marius as if to say, "Please."

Marius goes over to the mantel upon which is prominently displayed a glass cylinder with fine etchings. Inside is Marius' mother's collection of rocks. Marius hands Ira the glass, which is nearly full and quite heavy. The stones inside are indeed unique in color, size and variation. She tells us through Marius, "I have built up this collection over more than ten years." She invites Ira to sort through them and select any that he wants to photograph.

She has a story about each rock and remembers where she was and what year it was that she found it. It is apparent that she is very attached to this collection.

Ira asks Marius, "Are you sure she wants me to take them to photograph?"

"I-ra, I-ra, I-ra, it is no problem. Please take the rocks you want."

I pull Ira over to the side and whisper, "Are you sure you want to take these rocks? She seems really attached to them."

"Well, I don't think we can say 'no' now," Ira says.

"Hmm…. I remember someone telling me, 'It's easy, you just say 'no'," I reply.

Ira laughs. I laugh. And we are back to figuring out which rocks to take.

Ira carefully selects the ones he wants to use and Marius' mom hands him a few more, saying that these will look nice photographed, so he should take them as well.

There are over forty rocks of various shapes, sizes, and colors. We thank Marius' mom for the opportunity to meet her and for the rocks.

"I will take good care of them," Ira says. His plan is to photograph the rocks and return them to Marius' mom before we leave Lithuania.

I'm wondering how this is going to work, since we have only two days left.

We already have many things to do in our remaining time in Lithuania, including picking up our passports, visas, and other travel paperwork from the travel agent.

Marius has also asked Ira if he can do an additional photo shoot for his coffee business.

"How are you going to get it all done in time?" I ask Ira.

He looks at me with a confused expression.

"How are you going to get to photograph the rocks?" I ask more directly.

"Je-oanne, Je-oanne, we have time, Je-oanne, it is no problem," he replies in his Marius accent.

I have to wonder if it's going to be a problem, but I let it go.

We head to another town and spend a good part of the day photographing at Marius' coffee processing plant.

Coffee. Not rocks.

The two days fly by and we need to leave Lithuania to catch a train to Russia. Ira has run out of time to photograph the rocks.

"Marius, I am sorry," Ira says to Marius.

"Not a problem," Marius replies.

"I feel terrible after your mom was kind enough to let them into my care," Ira says.

"Don't worry, take the rocks to Russia and photograph them there."

"Are you sure it will not be a problem for your mom?"

"Ira, she will not mind," Marius replies.

I can't believe I am listening to this conversation. In addition to our backpacks, Ira's camera equipment, and laptop, we are now going to carry a bag of rocks into Russia? This does not make sense. But I guess in the name of art, what is sense?

∾

THE MORE THAN FORTY ROCKS WEIGH ABOUT SEVEN pounds. Ira tries to narrow the number down to a more mobile and, if possible, less ridiculous group. He separates the rocks into two piles, ones that he will take and ones that will not be leaving the safety of their home country.

I watch the separation process. And decide that I might as well be part of the process. I hand Ira a rock from the bigger pile. "You should take this rock. I think it will be good for the series," I say.

Ira gives me a quizzical look. "This is the pile that I'm taking," Ira replies.

"I thought you were only going to take a few?" I ask.

"Don't worry."

I'm worried. But I'm also laughing because this means Ira is going to be the one carrying the heavier pile of rocks into Russia.

Marius drives us to the train station. That might be enough for some people, but not Marius. He proceeds to get on the train to see us off. He is still on the train as it appears to begin to move.

I actually have a fleeting thought that maybe his mother told him that he had to keep his eyes on the rocks, and he is going to take the trip with us as their bodyguard. He gives us both a big Marius hug and finally gets off. He is standing on the platform waving to us with an enormous smile. A great man, indeed.

AFTER THE ROCK DISTRIBUTION, IRA'S "SKINNY" BAG OF rocks weighs at least seven pounds. We settle in for a good night's sleep and tuck in the rocks as they are traveling with us on the overnight train from Lithuania through Latvia and finally to St Petersburg, Russia.

We reach the border crossing from Latvia into Russia at midnight. Three stern Border Patrol Officers appear outside of our compartment. They wear stiff, formal military uniforms that communicate without words that this is about to get serious. Two of them come into our compartment and start banging with sticks at the benches we are sitting on and yelling at us in Russian.

We figure out that they want to check inside the benches, which are enclosed. They want to see if we are smuggling anyone into Russia. We open the lids, and they search the inside and confirm that there is no one else in our compartment. I have yet to make it into Russia, but I am not sure from what I have read and what I believe I know about Russia, coupled with this latest and first impression from these Russian border officers, why would anyone want to sneak into Russia. Sneak out, yes—sneak in, nyet!

As this is all happening, Ira lets me know that he begins to worry that the border officers will find the rocks. What if there is some restriction about bringing non-indigenous rocks into Russia and we will have to leave them at the border crossing between Latvia and Russia? He's already wondering how he is going to try to explain to Marius' mom that he had to surrender the rocks at the border and that she will have to pick them up in Latvia. No one would ever believe that one.

Just as Ira is finalizing the right words in his imaginary conversation with Marius' mom, the two of them finally leave our compartment and wait in the hallway for the final commanding officer.

If possible, the commanding officer is even colder than the last two guys. He gives a once-over at my passport and hands it back. Then he gives Ira a freezer-burn stare as he glares from his passport photo to his face, back again to him, and then back to his passport photo.

I can read the expression on Ira's face and it looks like this guy is making him nervous.

I know that Ira's passport photo was taken a few years ago and that in it he looks like a clean-cut Ron Howard as Opie Taylor from *The Andy Griffith Show*. Tonight, at midnight, he's not shaven, and he has long hair and a goatee. Oh, and did I forget to mention that we are smuggling rocks across the border?

Ira looks over at me through his sheer panic and gives me the "It's all going to be okay" look. Even though his expression looks like he is going to be physically dragged out of our compartment kicking and screaming, shouting, "Call the American Embassy when you get into Russia!"

On the train ride through Latvia, I checked for the four hundred-fiftieth time to ensure the Blue Envelope was still with me. It had become as important to me as my passport, airline tickets, and malaria medicine.

Finally, at midnight, the three of us passed through border control into Russia. The commanding officer stamps both of our passports and we are free to continue. We have finally made it safely, I believe, into Russia.

Our first stop in Russia is St. Petersburg; the Blue Envelope is almost at its final destination. Several days and an overnight train ride later, we arrive in Moscow.

Russia: If Only I Had a Hammer and Sickle

BANG!

Bang!

Bang!

A Russian woman pounds on the metal door to bring my breakfast. Morning coffee and toast is included in the apartment rental. I found this apartment by searching on the internet. I was thrilled when it turned out to be real. *Clang! Clang! Clang!* Louder and more intently each time. Then a flood of Russian words that I believe mean breakfast.

I hurry to unlock the two doors that separate us. I try with one of the two sets of duplicate keys that Ira and I were given when we arrived in Russia. First, I try the heavy key that looks like a remnant from the Czarist era. It turns. I open the first door and politely call, "One moment, please," to let the tray-bearer know I am on my way. I get to the second door. The remaining modern key won't turn. I try to force it. It doesn't budge.

I am literally trapped inside our fifth-floor temporary apartment in St. Petersburg.

Ira left this morning at six. to photograph the inside of the Metro stations just as they were opening. The stations are renowned for their ornate Art Deco style. Just yesterday, we took a guided walking tour. Part of the tour involved taking the Metro to different neighborhoods. We were in awe as we stood next to the massive mosaics depicting proletariat workers from the Communist era.

During one of our journeys through the Metro, Nikolai, our English-speaking Russian guide, saw Ira reach for his camera, preparing to take some pictures. Nikolai screamed in the tone of a KGB officer scolding someone who had just insulted Stalin, "Nyet! You are not allowed to photograph in Russian Metro stations! It is against the law, and you can get arrested!"

But Ira had to get the shot. "Is there someone of authority I can speak with?"

Nikolai exhaled a sigh, which I interpreted as, "Why is it so important for this New Yorker to photograph a train station anyway?" Reluctantly, after talking with several Metro workers, Nikolai finally got to speak face-to-face with the person in charge.

We waited patiently by the train tracks next to an aging booth still in use from the days of the Iron Curtain. Behind the closed doors, Nikolai and the Metro man-in-charge were having a heated Russian discussion. Although we had been in Russia for only a few days, it seemed that all conversations in Russian sounded heated—even if they were only about the weather. We tried to make out the words, but it was all Russian to us.

Eventually Nikolai reappeared. Apparently, this unnamed Metro monitor was perplexed by this request and told Nikolai, "Why would he want to get permission? It will take too long! There will be many forms to fill out! Just tell this man to come in at six in the morning tomorrow when no one is watching and simply sneak some shots." This is why Ira left early this morning and why I'm here trapped in the apartment.

Why an apartment in Russia? We decided that instead of staying in a hotel, we would try to experience the country as locals—though in a safe apartment. This apartment meets Ira's strict guidelines for safety mostly because it would be difficult for anyone to break in. It is in a courtyard off an alleyway on Nevsky Prospect, the "Fifth Avenue" of St.

Petersburg. In order to get in, someone—including us—needs to do the following:

1. Push open a large metal door and walk up one flight of stairs.
2. Enter a three-digit code to get past a door so solid that it must have been stolen from the Kremlin itself.
3. Climb up four more flights of stairs then knock on the third door to the left. The apartment maintenance man magically appears at any hour of day or night. Sometimes he appears before we knock. My theory is that he probably hears our heavy breathing as we climb the final flight.
4. Enter the main foyer. Now there are just two more doors to pass through to get into our apartment.
5. The first door, the metal one, answers to the modern key by opening into an entryway of our apartment. Only a hammer and sickle could penetrate this door.
6. The second door, by means of the czarist key, opens into our tiny studio. Both of these doors lock from the inside and the outside.

When Ira left this morning, he used his set of keys to lock the doors from the outside, leaving the second set of keys for me so I could get out—or so he thought.

Clang! Clang! Clang! What I can only assume is the Russian woman is outside my door persists. "Just a minute," I plead as I continue to fumble with the keys. She continues clanging, I continue fumbling. We are both losing our patience. I can hear her heavy sighs through the locked door. Suddenly, with a burst of clarity and remorse, I realize that some deranged Russian engineer designed this lock so that once it is locked from one side, it can only be opened from that side.

Still thinking clearly, I realize that the ever-present maintenance man will be able to set me free. I yell through the door, "Get the maintenance man! He will have a spare key!" Since I don't speak much Russian and she doesn't speak much English, we are getting nowhere.

I yell to her in English, and she yells back to me in Russian. Then I realize that the phrase "Get a spare key—I am locked **in**!" is not part of my *Lonely Planet* Russian phrasebook. As she storms away, I hear her footsteps pounding down the hallway, and I know that the only thing that is separating me from my morning thermos of hot coffee is this safe yet dysfunctional locking mechanism. Wait until I see Ira; I'll have a few choice phrases for him!

After a moment of growing regret that I won't be having my morning coffee, a slow panic sets in. "Oh no! I am trapped alone in a Russian apartment and have no way to get out!" I attempt to calm myself by thinking, "It's not so bad—I am safe *inside*, at least."

But it's no use, my mind starts racing with possibilities. What if Ira is gone all day? What if there is a fire? What if Ira is arrested, and I am the only one who can get him out? Then we will both be trapped, and neither of us able to help the other!

More bad news, there is no telephone in the apartment and my mobile phone doesn't work here. There isn't even a fire escape or a drainpipe to shimmy down. Anyway, would I have the courage to try it from the fifth floor?

I visualize what will happen if Ira is caught taking pictures. I am sure the police will ask to see his papers, want to extract a very expensive ruble fee, and possibly take him over to the station for a little one-on-one about the virtues of abiding by the laws. Ira will frantically try to explain to the police officer, "I was told by the man in the booth that I could take pictures if I came at six." I am pretty sure that this is not in the Russian phrasebook either. It occurs to me that it can truly be a lonely planet when you are locked in a room by yourself, and you think that the only person who can get you out is locked in a Russian prison.

By now, I am convinced that Ira is shackled and will be sent to Siberia. Suddenly the lock begins to turn. I stare at the door, expecting a giant Russian policeman.

The door squeaks open. Ira is standing there smiling. He balances two containers of coffee plus his precious set of keys. I can smell the coffee through the paper cups. "I took some great photographs at the Metro. Anything interesting happen here?" he asks.

"Nyet," I reply with a smile, "just waiting for my morning coffee."

I CALL THE NUMBER THAT SAMSINGH HAD GIVEN ME FOR Natasha. Surprisingly, it works! I introduce myself, tell her that I am a friend of Samsingh and that I have a letter for her. She suggests that we meet at Red Square at high noon. She describes what she looks like and I do the same.

"I think that might be her," I say to Ira as I see yet another woman who fits Natasha's description.

"Excuse me, are you Natasha?"

"Nyet."

"Excuse me, are you Natasha?"

"Nyet!"

And so it goes.

"Excuse me, are you Natasha?"

"Yes, I am."

Finally! I hand her the letter and explain how it found its way to her.

She stares at me in disbelief and says, "I am late for work. I will try to call you."

I watch her and the Blue Envelope walk away.

"THAT WAS FAST! WHAT HAPPENED?" IRA ASKS AS I RETURN to him with a shocked look.

I explain the lackluster response.

"That's it? No tears? No wedding invitation? No nothing?"

"Nyet, but she did say she would try to call."

"Try? Try to call?"

He hugs me, knowing that I was hoping for a better ending.

My heart feels hurt. Hurt from all the time and energy invested in this letter with nothing to show from it. I keep thinking about

Samsingh in his village wondering every day about how this will end.

Ira and I spent the day walking on the 500,000 square feet of red bricks in Red Square, admiring the brightly colored domes, towers, and spires of St. Basil's Cathedral, viewing fifteenth-century Russian artwork, and wondering what clandestine meetings are happening behind the walls of the Kremlin.

Later that evening, my phone rings. I quickly answer, hoping that it is Natasha. It is! She has late dinner plans and asks if I can meet afterward. She gives me the name and address and tells me to be there at midnight. Although it's later than I'd like to be out, I desperately want to have a different ending to this odyssey, so I accept her invitation.

I hang up and tell Ira where and when we are meeting. He offers to accompany me, in case it's a place that not even the Russian mafia would frequent. I am relieved to have his support and not have to meet this unknown woman in this unknown place alone.

Ira and I arrive at the designated meeting place to find a line-up of bouncers wearing tight black shirts and painted-on pants to accentuate their imposing bodies. We feel tiny next to these men built like skyscrapers. We approach them in hopes to enter, but only get back stares so icy they would make a Siberian winter seem warm. They gesture for our paperwork. We hand them our passports. They look at our pictures and then at us, mumble some undeterminable words, check our passports again, give each other a few looks, and finally let us pass.

The house music is pounding at decibels that would be illegal in America, the dance floor is packed, and disco balls reminiscent of *Saturday Night Fever* spin overhead. We squeeze our way past the dancing Muscovites, looking for Natasha. Again we find ourselves searching for her with no luck. But at least this time we know what she looks like!

We wait at a table near the door so we can hopefully see her enter. We sit in silence while we watch the people file in.

Then we see her stride through. We notice that the bouncers let her pass without looking at her papers.

"Hello!" we shout so she can hear us over the music.

"*Privet,*" she replies as she walks to our table.

She joins us and we talk about everything except the letter. We get to know about her life, her job, and her dreams for the future. She asks us about our journey, our time in Russia, and our relationship.

I'm just about to mention the letter when she asks if we want to dance. Seconds later we are dancing to song after song, which all sound the same to us. Eventually Natasha says she needs a break.

I ask Ira if he will get us some drinks, so I can have some time alone with Natasha. Since the bar is six people deep, I know we will have a lot of time. Natasha and I find a corner where we can hear each other speak.

"Thank you for your effort with the letter. You must be wondering about Samsingh and me," she says.

"Yes, a little," I reply, thinking that is the understatement of the year.

"He wooed me like no other man. We had blissful romantic nights in the desert. He made me feel like I was the most special woman in the world. When I was in India, I wished it could last forever."

"That all sounds wonderful, but I am sensing a 'however' coming."

"Yes, you are correct. However, being home made me realize how different our cultures were and that having a life together would not be possible. I also suspect that his proclaimed love for me was enhanced by the increase in quality of life he would have if we were together." She takes a deep breath and asks, "Do you think he was sincere?"

"His eyes lit up when he spoke about you; his smile went from ear to ear when he said your name. However, I too could not shake the feeling that it could have something to do with his thought of leaving his hard life in India."

We bond as if we are best girlfriends. She tells me that if I'm ever in Moscow again I can stay at her home. We hug each other, suspecting that we each could use one in that moment.

Russia: When the Kremlin Calls, Say "YES"

JULY 2005

We keep looking from our *Lonely Planet* guidebook to the map on the train trying to see the stop where we need to get off. Our heads are a bit fuzzy since we have just finished an overnight train ride from St. Petersburg.

Plus, the Metro stop names are in Russian, while our guidebook has them in English. We must look confused because a Russian man asks Ira, "You seem tense. Do you need help?"

"No, no. No, we're good," Ira says in order to brush him off, fearing that this guy is trying to set us up. We've had our share of people approaching us to scam us since we are foreigners and potentially easy targets.

"Where are you going?" he asks.

"The Kremlin," I say, blowing Ira's attempt to keep us safe in Moscow.

"I work at the Kremlin," he says. "Come, follow me."

We know that following strange men in Moscow is not the smartest idea, yet we are two steps behind him as we leave the Metro. I can see the panic in Ira's eyes as we realize that we have no idea where we are being taken. And then, we arrive at the Kremlin.

However, the entrance is barricaded off due to police activity.

"Oh, I guess today is not the right day for a tour," our new friend says.

We are partly bummed to miss out. And partly relieved since we still don't know if he's legit.

Ira and our friend—we decide to call him Mr. K.—exchange business cards and we say our goodbyes. The security guards wave Mr. K. right in. We look at his embossed business card and consider the fact that he got waved in and realize that he really does work there.

Ira and I find a place to discuss what just happened and to plot our next move in this big city. A few minutes later, Ira's flip phone rings. We're a bit shocked because no one has called us for months since they know we're traveling and international calling is super expensive. I hear Ira say, "I will have to check with Joanne and call you back."

"Who was that?" I ask.

"Mr. K.! He found out that some governmental thing is happening and public access to the Kremlin will be shut for a few days," Ira says. "And he can get us in. He wants to give us a private tour."

I appreciate how Ira wanted to check in with me, but I give him the authority to agree on my behalf the next time a call comes in from the Kremlin.

Ira calls Mr. K. back to determine the specific entrance where we are supposed to meet at one o'clock in the afternoon.

It's a bright sunny day and we're standing outside the Kremlin at the designated time, along with a dozen other tourists who have that confused look of wanting to get in and yet being unable to because of the barricade.

We see "our connection" through the iron gates. He is talking to a large stern security guard, gesturing with his hands over to where we are standing. Then they start to approach us. It's unclear from their expressions whether they are going to say, "Sorry, big mistake. You can't come in. Nyet," or "Welcome to the Kremlin."

They say neither, but the security guard says, "Come in."

The other tourists are looking at us with a "how did *they* get in?" expression as we work our way through the crowd.

We walk through the gates and suddenly there is no crowd. "Hello. Hello. Welcome to the Kremlin," Mr. K. says.

We look around in amazement—and a little shock—at the buildings, churches, and open expanse of the courtyard. Ira and I give each other the "how-did-we-get-here" look. And then we're off exploring.

"I'll show you around," Mr. K. says. "Oh, and feel free to take photos of anything, but please, take no photos of me."

We thank him for this opportunity and his generosity. He tells us not to worry about thanking him because he likes to practice speaking English.

"That's a lot of camera equipment you've got there," he says to Ira.

Ira typically doesn't want to tell people that he is a photographer for fear that they will rob him of the expensive gear he is traveling with. However, our guide has won over our trust. "Well, I am a professional photographer. Hoping to get some great photos of your country," Ira says.

As we walk past each building, Mr. K. gives us a detailed explanation of what we are looking at, the history behind it, and other facts that we wouldn't have known if we were doing this on our own. He lets us know that Kremlin means, "fortress inside a city" and is comprised of five palaces, four cathedrals and the Kremlin towers. It was established in 1482 and is the official residence of the Russian president.

We head into a church where a choir is performing in front of an empty congregation. Ira pops off photo after photo (not using flash, since that is one of the rules). Our guide tells Ira that he can hop over the rope if he wants to get closer. "But the rope is there to keep us out," Ira says.

"That is for the tourists. You are my special guest."

So Ira jumps over the rope and is in his glory, being so close to these magnificent relics. He is in photograph heaven, even for a Jewish guy capturing the magnificence of the cathedral, the artwork and the choir.

Then Ira hears yelling. In Russian. At him. The church caretaker appears out of nowhere, screaming at Ira to get back over the rope. Ira tries to explain that we have a personal escort, but that does not matter.

I imagine Russian guards taking Ira away for jumping the rope. And me trying to explain that we got permission from Mr. K. It's all falling short in my mind.

The church caretaker and Mr. K. exchange some heated words in Russian. Then the church monitor and Ira are able to work it out without anyone getting arrested. Ira hops back over the rope and all is good again in the world.

"I am sorry that happened," Mr. K. says.

"No, I'm sorry that I caused that to happen," Ira replies.

This goes on for a few iterations, until I interrupt, "Where to now?"

We walk and talk some more. About Russia. About the USA. About the Kremlin. About photography. And then Mr. K. announces abruptly, "I need to get back to work."

He walks us back to the gates and we say our goodbyes.

"Next time you are in Russia, look me up," he says.

"Next time you're in the United States, look us up," Ira and I reply in unison.

We walk out while waving goodbye to our new friend.

The kindness of strangers wins again.

IN SAINT PETERSBURG, I'VE VISITED SOME MUSEUMS AND train stations, and I've been locked inside an apartment.

What I haven't done is watch Ira taking photographs of Marius' mom's rocks. I guess the reason is that he has been too busy. So the rocks are coming with us on the overnight train. I hope he gets to photograph the rocks there.

Spain: Staying Safe at the Running of the Bulls

JULY 2005

WE LEAVE RUSSIA ON THE SCHEDULED DAY TO FLY TO Madrid to meet Trevor. When we land it's early evening and Trevor has already been in Madrid for a few hours. We drop our luggage at our hotel and rush off to meet him at the bar he said he'd be in. We try to call his mobile phone but have no luck getting through. We hope that he is at the designated spot. We hop in a cab looking forward to seeing a familiar face after all these months.

After we arrive at our meeting spot, we walk in and look around for him. It's a crowded, loud place. No sign of Trevor.

"What should we do?" I yell at Ira.

"Let's wait outside," he yells back.

We are standing in the street looking for our friend. Lots of partiers are passing us by. Just then we see a bachelorette party with the bride wearing a sash indicating she is the one getting married.

And then, in the middle of the party, we see him.

"Trevor!" I scream, waving my hands frantically.

"J-Fly!" he yells back, using the nickname he calls me. "I-ra!" he yells, sounding out Ira's name like a cheer.

He breaks away from the bachelorette and runs to us. We're

hugging and jumping up and down like maniacs or really great friends who have not seen each other in four months.

The bachelorette party is waiting for Trevor to come back to them. "Sorry, my friends are here now so I need to run. Was great hanging out with you."

We hear a collective groan from the women.

"Only you can be in Spain for a few hours and wind up with a bachelorette party," Ira says.

"Hey man, my nickname is Circus. Everywhere I go, there is a party. Who wants paella?" Trevor says.

We both say, "Me!"

And we're off to find the best paella in Madrid.

WE STAY IN MADRID FOR ONE NIGHT AND THEN GRAB OUR rental car to drive to Pamplona. The home of the Running of the Bulls.

"Are you sure you want to run with the bulls, T-Rev?" I ask, using the nickname I call him.

"J-Fly, I came all the way out here to run with the bulls. Why would I change my mind now?"

"I don't know. Because it's super dangerous and you can die. Isn't it enough to just be in Pamplona and watch?"

"I swam with sharks on all but one continent. I do shit like this," he says.

"Yeah, I know. I know," I say. I just don't want my friend to get hurt or die.

WE ARRIVE IN PAMPLONA AT NIGHT AND IMMEDIATELY HIT the streets which are teeming with soon-to-be-runners and those who are there just to party. The town is electric with excitement. Tons of people everywhere. We're in a local shop and Trevor and the local shopkeeper strike up a conversation.

"How long have you been living in Pamplona?" Trevor asks.

"My whole life, fifty-seven years," the shopkeeper responds.

Trevor asks what seems like the obvious next question. "Have you run with the bulls?"

"Are you insane? Have you seen the size of them? They are huge!" he replies while gesturing with his hands.

I know from my research that the bulls can weigh up to 1,300 pounds. I hope that this local may change Trevor's mind, but he seems unfazed.

We continue out in the street and join the scene of partiers.

We meet an Australian man who tells us he has been coming to Pamplona for the past fifteen years and has run with the bulls fourteen of those years.

Ira and Trevor inside the corrida at the Running of the Bulls (Pamplona, Spain). Photo credit: Joanne Flynn Black

"Number one: if you get knocked down, stay down. Bulls will try to avoid something in the road if they can," he says.

"Seems logical," Ira replies.

"Number two: to reinforce number one, don't try to get up. When you get up is when you are a target for the bull to charge at," he continues.

"How will you know when to get up?" Trevor asks.

"I was just getting there, mate. And number three: when you get knocked down, stay down until someone comes along and taps you on the shoulder and tells you it's safe to get up. Bulls don't talk so you will know this is the right timing."

Primed with this inside scoop from someone who has successfully survived the bulls, Trevor is as ready as he'll ever be.

We continue drinking.

The next morning, we wake up early. Ira is his usual chipper self, first thing in the morning. I'm having a harder time getting up.

I'm half hoping that Trevor changed his mind, and we can go back to sleep.

I hear Ira saying to Trevor in the other room, "Trev, Trev, come on, man. It's time."

I can hear Trevor's mumble from a groggy response coming through the walls. Oh, I think, maybe he's hung over and doesn't want to run. And then he must have popped out of bed because now I can hear him loud and clear.

"J-Fly! Come on! We can't be late!"

I'm not sure how we did it but minutes later we're walking down the streets of Pamplona in our red scarves, white shirts, white pants, and red sashes. The "uniform" that everyone, literally everyone, is wearing.

Ira and I get a prime spot atop a pole to watch the runners. He's set with his camera to capture the moment. I'm having the time of my life people watching and talking with others who are there to watch a friend run.

And then it starts. People are running. Bulls are charging. There's an energy of scared excitement in the air. People yelling. I feel this to my core. Yes, they are excited they are also fearful. Some of these people may lose a loved one if they get gored by a bull. Or if not killed, they would wind up in a hospital seriously injured. The course runs along an enclosed stretch of about a half-mile through several narrow streets of the old quarter of Pamplona.

It's a frenzy of screams with people running and bulls running and dangerous corners.

We hear someone shout that the final bull has passed, and we should run to the *corrida* (aka the bullring) to watch the action before they close the doors. We somehow didn't realize that this was going to happen, but we want to be part of the action. So, Ira and I run down the streets heading to the corrida. We're panting as we make it through the gates seconds before they close. We are safe in the stands while the runners are in the middle of the ring with the bulls.

"Wow, that was intense!" I say to Ira. "So glad that Trevor made it."

"Yes. Yes," he says with a faraway look.

He's watching all the men in the corrida with the bulls and I realize it's not over.

"Trevor's in there with the bulls?" I ask.

"Yeah, seems like it," he says.

"That's kinda crazy. I'm glad we're here in the stands and safely away from the bulls," I say.

"Uh-huh," Ira says. And I realize what he's thinking. I can see it in his eyes.

"I'm going to go out there and photograph," he says.

"You're what?"

"I'm going to find Trevor and get some shots of him. I'll be safe."

"How can you be so sure of that?" I ask. But I know it's a lost cause. It's the perfect place for amazing photos.

"Okay, try to stay away from the bulls," I say. And give him a kiss as he hops the ring and is in the middle of the action.

I'm watching as close as I can to see that Ira and Trevor are safe. I'm feeling pretty smug that I'm the smartest one of us three, safe on the outside of the ring in the stands. I watch as Ira is taking photos of people who are very close to the bulls. Too close for my liking.

I hear people screaming and look inside the ring to make sure Ira and Trevor are far away from any bulls, yet I cannot figure out why everyone is screaming.

I notice that while I am looking inside the ring, the people on the inside are looking at me. I glance to my right and realize that a bull has jumped over the wall of the ring and is headed towards me. Straight towards me. There is nowhere to run.

Just then, Ira is charging towards me. I'm paralyzed with fear about what to do next. Ira reaches me and pulls me over into the ring just as the bull passes where I was standing.

"You okay?" he asks.

I look at him and laugh, realizing that after all my worrying about Trevor running and him photographing, I am the one who almost got run over by a bull. I'm scared yet exhilarated. A bit shaken. I checked myself to see if I was scraped anywhere.

Just then Trevor runs over to us. "J-Fly, that bull was really close to you."

"I know! And he was large!"

"Really large," Trevor says, gesturing with his hands.

We laugh. "Want to get out of here?" Ira says.

"I think we need a beer," I say. And we walk out of the corrida. Three amigos who came a little too close to the bulls.

"WHAT WAS IT LIKE TO PHOTOGRAPH?" I ASK IRA WHEN we're safely at a bar away from any bulls.

"It's something to watch people running from a bull. There is a certain sense of urgency, and panic or terror the closer they are to the bull," he says.

He explains that there's a series of images he's calling, "Waiting for the Other Shoe to Drop."

"Why is that?" I ask.

"Because the guy I am photographing was hit by the bull and hoisted in the air. His shoe was knocked off. It takes four frames of images for his shoe to actually hit the ground. During this time, he is still being hoisted by the bull. Crazy!"

I can see the excitement when Ira is describing this. It must be a photographer's dream to catch this in action.

I look over at Trevor and see how happy he is that he successfully was able to complete this. I ask how he's feeling now that he's finished.

"Finished?" he asks.

"Yeah, finished. You came. You ran. What else is there to do?"

"I'm going to run tomorrow too," he says.

"Tomorrow?" I ask. And I'm just about to protest and ask what for. And then I realize how much he gets from this adrenaline and I say, "Glad I bought two white shirts."

We toast to the bulls and to Trevor for being brave enough to run and a friend enough to come halfway around the world to meet us.

I think it is also worth mentioning that in Pamplona we have seen Trevor run with the bulls two times, and we have seen bulls jumping into the stands, but what we have not seen is Ira photographing Marius' mom's rocks!

TREVOR'S TIME WITH US ENDS, AND IRA HAS STILL NOT photographed the rocks.

Ira and I are at the internet cafe in Sevilla and I hear him say, "Uh-Oh," and let out a deep breath when he opens his email messages.

"What is it, babe? Are our parents okay?" I say, hoping it's not health related.

"No, they are fine. It's an email from Marius."

"Oh. Everything okay with Jolita and the baby? "

"Yeah, yeah, she's good. It's just that...." and Ira trails off.

"What is it?"

"Marius' mom keeps asking if I've mailed the rocks back yet."

"Of course she does. She loves those rocks."

"I know. It gets worse."

"How can it get worse? I don't know what you mean. Did she send a search party out for them?"

"Marius is tired of her asking about the rocks every time he calls her. So he's stopped calling her."

"Oh man. That is just wrong. You've got to get the rocks back to her."

Since leaving Deloitte Consulting, one of the thoughts I've had about what I should do next in my life is to run a consulting firm focused on helping woman-owned small businesses. Although Ira is not a woman, I decide to assist him, as he appears to be in dire need of some serious Project Management help. Shooting the rocks becomes the project and I share with Ira a three-phased project plan to complete the shooting.

I draw out my plan. It includes:

- Phase 1: when the rocks will be photographed.
- Phase 2: when they will be mailed back to Lithuania.
- Phase 3: the final stage is represented by a colored smiley face to illustrate Marius' mom when she and the rocks are safely reunited.

I throw in an added drawing of Ira before Phase 1 and he is a stressed-out mess, aka the current state. At the completion of the project, he is smiling almost as much as Marius' mom.

There is a wrench in my plan, however. We have found ourselves at the southern tip of Spain and about an hour's ferry ride from Morocco. We've wanted to go to Morocco for a long time and it will be hard to be so close and not go there.

We are weighing the pros and cons of going to Morocco when I say, "You are not taking the rocks to Morocco!"

The rocks are starting to come between us. They represent a weight, a heaviness in the interest of the relationship, Ira decides that the rocks need be photographed in Spain and then shipped before we head on the ferry to Morocco. We agree that once the rocks are shot, we will head to Morocco.

The next morning, Ira heads to the post office to finally return the rocks. They are still unphotographed -- but at least they will make it back to Marius' mom. I feel bad that Ira didn't get to photograph them but really? It's been way too long.

Ira comes back from the post office with the rocks still in his hands.

"Wait, what happened?"

"The post office is on holiday and will be for another three days," Ira says.

"I don't understand. There wasn't a box that you could drop them in?"

"Apparently not."

We're both not happy about the situation.

I can see how stressed Ira looks. Maybe he was expecting me to say I was going to Morocco without him or the rocks.

I look at Ira and smile, "I guess the rocks are coming to Morocco."

The Rocks En Route to Morocco

JULY 2005

As we're getting on the ferry from Spain to Morocco, Ira carries his backpack, his camera bag, his laptop, and a bag with the rocks. The bag with the rocks has now traveled from Lithuania to St Petersburg, from St Petersburg to Moscow, from Moscow to Spain, and from Spain, it's heading to Morocco.

At this point the double thick plastic bag is barely holding together, and at the exact moment that Ira steps onto the gangplank of the ferry, it begins to break apart. In a movement that combines the balance and grace of a Baryshnikov with the sheer brute strength of Hercules, Ira tries to stop the forces of nature and stave off the terror that is about to happen.

He is able to catch the bottom of the bag just as the rocks are about to plunge into the Straits of Gibraltar, where they will be lost forever. He is able to perform this feat without losing a single rock. I witness all of this. I'm shocked.

"I can't believe what I just saw," I say to Ira.

"Yeah, that was close. Really close."

We get on the ferry and settle into a seat on the upper deck. Ira says nothing, he's just breathing heavy.

"That. Was. Really. Close," I say again.

I then offer Ira one of my "My Own Bags," which have been designed by our friend Ania. This bag has been with us for the past four months and has withstood my rigorous treatment and the extreme weight I have stuffed into it.

"You're sure I can have this?" Ira asks.

"I just want the rocks to be safe so they can get back to Lithuania."

"I am sure the rocks will be safe in their new home and that the bag will not rip, break, or tear. I might actually have a chance to photograph them."

"Yes, like today. And then you will mail them."

"I feel that since so much time has gone by and after carrying the rocks through so many countries, I am feeling the pressure that the shots need to be of a quality that is beyond exceptional," Ira says.

"There is no pressure, just shoot the rocks," I say.

We arrive in Casablanca and decide that the rocks need to be shot here as we believe it will be harder to mail as we head farther into Morocco. And come on—it's about time. There can be no more distractions. Shooting the rocks takes precedence. We head to the beach and try to get to one of the entrances. The attendants want us to pay for the full day even though it's 3 pm.

"Want to find another way onto the beach?" Ira asks.

"Let's just spend a few minutes, shoot the damn rocks, and get out," I say.

We find an entrance that is not guarded. We walk on the beach and find a good area to begin photographing. Things seem to be looking up, for a moment. Then a local Moroccan man decides to take an interest in what we are up to. He looks a bit disheveled with ripped jeans and sandals. He doesn't look like he belongs on the beach. He comes up to us and starts chatting us up. "What are you doing?" he asks.

Ira answers with evident disinterest, hoping that his lack of eye contact will convince him to just be on his way.

"You are so pretty," he says to me.

I start to get a bit nervous. Of course, because we're in the unguarded area far away from the other area, it feels like no one will hear us even if we scream.

"You are so pretty," he says to me.

Ira looks at me with his "this photo shoot is over" look.

"Get behind me," Ira says to me.

Persistently, this man is still making comments about how he would be a better boyfriend for me.

I'm worried about us. I'm worried about Ira's camera equipment. And I'm worried about the rocks. We've got to get them and get out of here.

Ira tells me to run away. Ira begins holding his camera like a weapon so that if this guy comes too close, he will clock him with the body, or the lens, or his fist, if necessary, anything to keep him away.

We pick up the rocks and begin to run.

He is screaming at us, but he is not following.

We have gotten away safely.

We head back to our hotel room and try to wash off the experience.

This is the first time in our entire trip that we have felt so close to danger. "That was scary," I say.

"Yeah, shook me a bit," Ira says. "You okay?"

"Yes, just a bit shaken. You?"

"Feeling the same."

"Did you get enough photos of the rocks?" I ask.

"I did. I'm ready to mail them back. Phase 1 of your plan is complete."

"That's good."

The next day, Ira heads to the post office in Casablanca with his "My Own Bag" of rocks ready to be mailed. I stay back at the hotel and enjoy some coffee while he's off to finish this saga.

The hotel has newspapers in English and I'm flipping through them when Ira returns.

"So?" I say.

"The rocks have been mailed," Ira replies.

"Oh, thank God. I'm so happy they are gone."

Ira looks a bit hurt. "I mean, I'm so glad they are on their way back to their rightful owner."

"Yeah, so am I," Ira replies.

"How was it at the post office? Did they want to know what you were mailing?"

"It turned out well, but at the beginning, there was some confusion about the name of the country and how it translated. We went back and forth a few times with some folks, but we finally figured it out.

"I guess they don't have lots of people sending mail from Casablanca to Lithuania." I was going to sarcastically add mailing rocks, but I decided this wasn't the right time for sarcasm.

"I'm going to send Marius a note letting him know that the rocks are in the mail," Ira says.

"Babe. I'm glad this rock saga is behind us," I say.

He sighs and agrees.

Gibraltar: The Rock

AUGUST 2005

WE'RE ON OUR LAST NIGHT IN MOROCCO AND I'M checking the schedule for the ferry back to Spain. And then I see it. And I stare for a moment. I go into that travel planning trance I find myself in sometimes. *Hmm..*

Ira notices. He looks at me.

"So, I was thinking…," I say.

"Uh-oh, that usually gets us in trouble," Ira says with a smile.

"We're really close to Gibraltar…."

"And what's in Gibraltar?"

"Well, for one, the rock."

"Yes, and…?"

"I'm not sure what else, but wouldn't it be cool to go and see what it's like? When else are we going to go to Gibraltar?" I say.

"But why would we want to go to Gibraltar?" he says.

"It's really small. The whole place is less than three square miles. We can practically walk it!" I say.

"Really, it's that small?"

"Yeah, what I was reading says two point six square miles. Most of it is comprised of the rock. You have a thing for rocks," I say with a smile.

"That is true. Ahh, why not?" Ira says.

And with that, I'm checking the ferry options to Gibraltar.

The next day we leave from Tangier, Morocco, and head to the British territory of Gibraltar. I really have no idea what it's like there. I only know it's famous for a rock. I see it on the ads for Prudential.

When the ferry docks, we find cobblestone streets that are filled with pubs. And people who seem to be enjoying themselves in those pubs and on those streets. Because we've been surrounded by so many different cultures, it's a bit of a culture shock to suddenly be thrown in with folks who look like Londoners.

Spain has been trying to take control of this small piece of land for centuries because whoever owns it controls the Strait of Gibraltar. It's an area that is only nine miles wide yet half of the world's shipping trade passes through it. I can see why it's an important piece of land.

We have fish and chips for lunch. Having just come from Morocco, we feel really odd to be eating greasy English food. But we enjoy the familiarity of it.

"Should we go check out what the fuss is about this rock?" Ira asks.

"Let's do it."

We get our tickets for the rock. It's a six-minute gondola ride to get to the landing point.

When we get to the top, we're impressed with how high up we are and with the natural beauty. Like being on top of a mountain that you plan to ski down.

"I can see why people say 'solid as the rock of Gibraltar,'" I say.

"Yeah, it's pretty massive."

"You know what would make this experience better?" I ask.

"Better? What could make it better?"

"If we still had Marius' mom's rocks. They would photograph really well up here," I say with a serious face.

Ira's about to agree with me and then catches the joke.

"I kinda miss the rocks," he says.

"I kinda miss them too," I say.

Back in Spain: The Rocks

BACK IN SPAIN, IN WORKING THROUGH THE LOGISTICS OF one our last legs of the trip we stop by a travel agency office.

We notice an atlas on the travel agent's shelf and ask if we can see it. She hands it over to us. I'm checking out distances and locations of different options. The names of countries are in Spanish or another language and they are spelled differently than we are used to, but we can mostly make them out.

"Oh shit!" Ira says abruptly.

"What is it?"

"Letonia! Letonia!" Ira points to the place on the map and tells me in an extremely frantic tone, "Letonia is the spelling that the Moroccan post office thought was for Lithuania."

"What?"

"Letonia is not Lithuania. It's Latvia. Baby, I am sure that the rocks are now on the way to Latvia and not Lithuania."

"Oh shit. You are right. What do you think will happen to the rocks?

"Well, I guess they could still be sitting in a Latvian Post Office while they try to figure out what to do with them," Ira says.

"Or the Latvian post office has already decided that there is no such address in Latvia, figured out that it is Lithuania and have forwarded them on to Lithuania," I say.

"Or the Latvian post Office has decided that there is no such address in Latvia and have decided to ship the rocks back to the shipper, which is me and my address back in New Jersey," Ira says.

I imagine Ira returning home to a bag of rocks.

"Oh no. Or the Latvian post office has decided that there is no such address in Latvia and have decided to ship the rocks back to the shipping Post Office, which is Casablanca," Ira says. "In this case, the rocks are currently sitting in the Casablanca post office until someone comes to claim them."

"We are not going back to Morocco to claim the rocks," I say.

"I must have had rocks in my head to take the rocks out of Lithuania," Ira says.

"Sorry babe. This is not good," I say.

"I'm not sure if Marius' mom and her rocks will ever see each other again."

"You have to tell Marius," I say.

"I don't think an email will do for this one. I'm going to have to call him.

"Good luck, babe."

Spain: Saying Goodbye

AUGUST 2003

THE NEXT DAY WE HEAD TO BARCELONA. WE SPEND A FEW days there and check out the things Barcelona is famous for, including the Gaudi buildings and churches. Then we reach the point in our trip where we're supposed to part ways. I'm going on to Italy, but Ira's plan is to skip Italy and go home directly from Spain.

I'm not exactly sure why he formed this plan, but I think the psychology of being gone for six months had something to do with it. When we were planning the trip, his brother Steve had said, "Six months? Six whole months! You're going to be gone for half a year."

Also, being away from home and burning through all of our money has played a role. The need for a job is weighing heavy on him. And I imagine also figuring out what we are going to do with our relationship is on his mind. And meeting my entire Italian family is probably something he's not sure he wants to do since he isn't sure where our relationship is headed.

My flight for Italy is in one week. I don't really want to stay in Barcelona for the whole time, but I need to stay close by so Ira can catch his flight home from Barcelona. I'm reading the *Lonely Planet* guide when I see a mention of a town only a train ride away that is on the beach.

"Hey, I think I've seen all I need to see in Barcelona," I say to Ira. "Plus, I'm not sure this is where I want to be my first week of being solo before I head to Italy."

"Yeah, it might not be the safest place," Ira replies. "Did you want to head off and start your Italy trip sooner?"

"What?"

"You know, leave me here and head to Italy?"

"No, I don't want to leave you."

"What should we do?"

"Well, I was reading about this cool beach town which is not too far from here. It's called Sitges. It's predominantly a gay town."

"A gay town?"

"A town where lots of gay people vacation."

"Is that where you want to spend your last week?"

"Let's try it out."

And just like that we're packing up our backpacks and researching the train schedule to head to a town neither one of us has heard about before.

THE TRAIN RIDE IS A QUICK FORTY-FIVE MINUTES, YET WE feel like we've entered another world. Gone are the towering Gaudi spires and ornate buildings from Barcelona. We're surrounded by low buildings and the beach.

We find a clean, modest apartment that is not far from the beach and settle in.

While in Sitges, Ira and I enjoy being at the beach, eating seafood, and just relaxing. But Ira's looming departure is with us like an unwanted traveling partner.

It's hard to fully relax when we know that pretty soon, we will be apart.

The day of his flight home arrives.

"I'm going to miss you, babe," I say.

"Nah, you're going to have a solo adventure, like you always wanted," Ira replies.

"It's not going to be the same without you," I say.

"Yeah, you'll have more fun," Ira says with a smile. "I'm going to miss you too, babe."

We say our teary goodbye. I wave him off.

As he leaves, I'm not sure how I'll make it a whole month without him. I know that I planned to take this trip solo. But now, after spending every waking and sleeping moment with Ira, being solo doesn't seem important anymore.

I'M NOT SURE WHAT TO DO, SO I HEAD TO AN OUTDOOR CAFE and watch all the people walking by. Everyone is looking so spectacular. It's almost like being at a parade in the Castro district of San Francisco.

In fact, the whole scene reminds me of living in San Francisco, but in a beach town. I start to imagine what it would be like if my friends Allison and Eddy were here. The people watching would be way more fun if I had someone to watch with.

I'm also missing Ira and thinking about what it would be like if he was next to me enjoying an espresso.

Then the guy at the table next to me sees my *Lonely Planet* guidebook and says, "Excuse me, I see you are reading a book that is in English. Do you speak English?"

"Yes," I say.

"I moved here from the United States to be near my boyfriend. Everyone speaks Spanish of course. I would love to talk to someone in my native language," he says. "It's not easy to have to translate everything in your mind every time you say or hear something."

"That must be difficult," I say.

And then we continue chatting.

Before you know it, I'm meeting his boyfriend and his friends. And we're spending every day and night together for a week. Visiting Gaudi parks, going to gay clubs, and enjoying a new-found friendship.

Italy: Mia Famiglia in Piacenza

SEPTEMBER 2005

I ARRIVE VIA TRAIN FROM MILAN TO PIACENZA. MY UNCLE Luigi and cousins Manuela and Valentina are there to greet me at the train station. There's lots of hugs and double kisses. And ciaos. It's the first time we are meeting. Other than my Grandma Rose, I'm the first relative to visit from America.

They drive in their little FIAT to their house, where my aunts are waiting for me sitting on their porch.

I'm taken aback by how my aunt Luisa reminds me of my Aunt Eleanor. And my Uncle Luigi reminds me of my Uncle Richie.

It makes sense to have such close resemblances, since my grandma Rose was the sister of both of their moms.

My grandma Rose came to America with the plan that her parents would eventually "send for the sisters" when they had enough money. But that never happened. She had five children of her own, Ronald, Eddie, Joseph (my dad), Richie, and Eleanor. And a husband who died young.

She raised them by working at the church. The kids would chip in by taking jobs around town like delivering the local newspapers and shining shoes.

I'm snapped back to the porch by the family handing me presents, including a handknit shawl and slippers. I accept them graciously. My cousin Valentina is the youngest and the one who speaks the best English. She's acting as a translator for us as we get to know each other better.

Every morning I come downstairs to a table full of breakfast items. My aunts make espresso for me in a traditional Biagliatti, an on-the-stove espresso pot. They note what I like and what I don't. The next day only the things I like appear. Since they don't speak English and my Italian is only a handful of phrases, our morning conversation consists of lots of pointing and yumms.

Every day they take me to see some other relative. I didn't realize how many cousins and aunts and uncles I have over here.

Italy: Mozzarella, Michelangelo, and George Clooney

SEPTEMBER 2005

"Andiamo! Andiamo!" I DO NOT SPEAK MUCH ITALIAN, BUT I know that phrase. The other passengers shout, "Move it!" as they push past me. We are on the ferry from Stresa to Isla Bella on Lake Maggiore, Italy.

"Mi scusi, scusi, fotographia," I plead as I point to my camera to let them know that I'm simply trying to take a photo. I want to see the islands we are navigating past on our way toward our final destination. The problem is that I'm neither getting on nor off until the last stop, so I'm repeatedly mashed in the middle of people.

It's no use. I'm sandwiched like a piece of mozzarella cheese with a backpack between two slices of Italian bread. People coming on are pushing me toward the back wall. People getting off are pushing me toward the outside ramp. Most of my pictures are turning out to be of the backs of people's heads as they push me out of the way.

I think back on the reason why I am here.

Previously, I was in Milan. Right in the middle of the summer. The heat was melting my gelato faster than I could eat it. It was time to get out of the city and head to the cooler areas of the north. With several lakes to choose from, I decided to ask a local for a recommendation.

"Which lake is the best?" I asked the front desk attendant at my hostel, who looked like Elvira's twin.

"Ahh, well, Lake Maggiore is the most breathtaking of all the lakes in Italy, but Lake Como is where George Clooney lives," she replied with a dreamy look, batting her eyelashes as if it were George Clooney in front of her.

I decided that a George Clooney sighting at Lake Como was probably quite rare, so I packed my backpack and boarded the next train to Lake Maggiore.

In the middle of the summer in Italy, it seemed like everyone had the same idea. The train was crowded with families from Milan trying to escape the heat. My backpack was stored on my lap due to the overhead storage area being overstuffed with Louis Vuitton wheelie bags. On top of this, the air conditioning was blowing out warm air. Although the heat was unbearable, I tried to concentrate on the view of the Italian countryside.

The train passed through towns with rolling hills and homes perched high among the trees. Although I was surrounded by many people, I felt alone. I played "I'm Just a Girl in the World" by No Doubt on my iPod to combat my loneliness.

Arriving at Lake Maggiore, I was ready to enjoy the fresh mountain air. Longing for a breeze, I decided to take one of the many ferries I saw heading to different islands on the lake. I stopped by the tourist office to look at the schedule.

Choosing a destination and deciphering the ferry schedule seemed as complicated as the traffic flow in Rome. I looked around for someone who could explain the schedule to me, but everyone was busy helping customers, smoking a cigarette, or sipping an afternoon espresso.

It looked like it might take as long to get help as it took for the Sistine chapel to be completed. I decided I would buy a ticket for whichever ferry was leaving next and let fate lead me. The ferry I chose had a final destination of Isla Bella, an island filled with gardens, grottos, and peacocks, at least according to my guidebook.

My plan was to sit on the upper deck and feel the breeze blowing through my hair like in a scene from a movie. As I was envisioning this, the ferry arrived. I lugged my backpack down the ramp and onto the boat. Finally, as I was getting on board, I felt a slight breeze. I took this deep into my lungs, thinking things were finally starting to go my way. I was beginning to gain confidence as a solo female traveler.

Upon boarding, I walked all the way around to look for a door that opened up to the deck. After circling the entire boat, I realized there was no "outside." The ferry was completely enclosed by glass. It wasn't even clean clear glass. The glass looked like it was frosted to prevent people from seeing out. As I got a closer look, I realized that the "frosting" was simply dirt and fog. I thought to myself, "This is not possible." I could not believe I had left the heat of Milan only to be on a fully enclosed submarine above the water.

Disappointed, I settled into a seat and pressed my face against the hard glass to try to see something. Anything!

The ferry had several stops along the lake before it reached Isla Bella. With each stop a transfer of bustling passengers occurred. Each time the door opened to let people on or off, I made my move to position myself by the door to get a breeze and snap a few photographs of the towns we were passing.

This is where the shouting began. *"Andiamo! Andiamo!"*

I am, however, determined to get some air. The next time the door opens, I go through the same push-and-shove routine. This time, I notice the ferryboat captain, a very stern and weathered-looking man, staring at me in disbelief. I know from the various countries I've traveled through that there are many restrictions on taking photographs of train stations, airports, and other methods of transportation. Hello, Russian Metro!

I wonder if the Italian ferries have similar laws that I'm breaking right in front of the captain.

No sooner have I finished my thought than the ferry captain marches over to me. He yells something I cannot understand in rapid-fire Italian and gestures for me to follow him.

Oh, no! This is not good.

It's my first day alone and already I'm going to get arrested! My first thought is, "Make a break for it." I can run off the ramp and be free. The captain will never be able to catch me. There's one flaw in my plan, however. I have my backpack, and it will be pretty easy for him to catch us both.

Resigned to whatever will be my newfound fate, I follow the captain with my head down. Passengers in their seats stare at us as we pass by. It's not looking good.

He turns the corner and opens a hobbit-sized door. We climb steps so small I wonder how a hobbit could fit – never mind the captain. I sidle up the steps and at the top realize that we are now at the bridge. He points towards the open door and makes a "click-click" gesture with his hands.

"*Fotographia!*" he exclaims as he points again to the small deck outside. Then I realize that he isn't bringing me up to put me in the brig, but to let me take photos from the only place on the ferry that has an open door.

I walk to the ledge and breathe in the clean air. I feel the breeze blow through my hair. Ahhh. This is what I wanted.

"*Scusi, signorina,*" the captain and his second officer say, as they join me on the deck. Without the barrier of the frosted glass, I'm able to see the clear water, the hillside homes, and the majestic mountains. Off to the left, we see islands sprinkled throughout the lake.

What I earlier thought was the stern demeanor of the captain now looks more like the face of a proud father. He gestures at the mountains, the water, and the boats.

Then he asks me, "*Bellisimo, non?*"

I agree, "Beautiful." He starts doing the "click-click" motion again and I understand that he's allowing me to take a picture with him. His

Joanne and Ira driving the ferry boat (Lake Maggiore, Italy).

second officer takes the camera and I stand next to the proud captain. He takes off his captain's hat and lets me wear it for the photo.

We hear the ferry driver calling us. Moving toward the driver's seat, I think he wants his picture taken. But no! He wants to let me drive the ferry! Getting up from his seat, he gives me control of the helm.

While guiding the ferry, I contemplate that being "a girl alone in the world" can make some interesting experiences possible. Still wearing the captain's hat, I drive the ferry across the lake, keeping an eye out for George Clooney.

Maybe George wants to see the beauty of Lake Maggiore today also. I am pretty sure he won't get to drive a ferry.

Home

I'M BACK HOME.

But home isn't really home.

San Francisco was really my home. Where all the relationships I'd built over the last ten years of my life were. And now I'm in Morristown, New Jersey. Living in Ira's house. Well, actually half of a house. He's still renting out the other half to help pay the mortgage.

Ring.

Ring.

Ring.

"Ira, could you get that? I don't want to talk to anyone," I say.

I hear Ira answering the questions from the person on the other side of the phone. "She's good…. A bit tired…. Her favorite country? I think it was India. Yes, she'll call you back."

And so it goes for a week.

"You're going to need to start talking to people pretty soon, you know?" Ira says to me.

"Yeah, I know. I'm just not ready yet."

I'm not sure why I can't talk to people. I just can't.

Ira and I are trying to find our grounding. Since we're in half of a house, we turn the former laundry room into a makeshift kitchen. We buy a refrigerator which is slightly larger than the college dorm version.

We both have no jobs, no money, no direction. Worst of all, we're not in travel mode where we were moving to a different location every three days.

We are standing still.

And there is no *Lonely Planet* to guide us to our next stop.

This all culminates with "the conversation."

We're sitting inside Panera Bread in what I think is a lunch out to get away from the house.

"I don't think I can continue going on like this," Ira says.

"We're going through a tough time because we're just used to being on the road. And now we're figuring stuff out," I say. "It will get better."

"I don't think I can continue going on like this," Ira says again.

"Wait, are you breaking up with me?" I ask.

"I think it's for the best," Ira says.

"The best? The best for who?" I ask.

"For both of us," Ira replies.

I'm sitting here in shock. I can't believe that after all of this time together on the road it's coming down to this.

"But...." I start to cry.

Right in the middle of Panera Bread.

I think about all the adventures of the trip. I can't help but feel pissed that I shared all of these memories with someone who is no longer going to be in my life.

I also can't help but find it ironic that instead of "breaking bread" at Panera Bread, Ira is breaking up with me here.

Where to next?

It's obvious that I can't stay living with Ira in our half a house. But where to go? I don't want to move in with my parents. That would seem like two steps back. And I'm not in the financial situation to rent my own place.

I decide to call Trevor to ask about his country house. His mom lives in New York City right across the street from the Washington Square arch. She only visits the country house occasionally.

"Hey Trev."

"Hey. I'm really sorry to hear about you and Ira. What is wrong with that boy?" he says.

"I know, I ask myself that question daily. That is sorta why I'm calling. I have a question."

"Sure. Ask away," he replies.

"Do you think you and your mom would be okay if I stayed in your country house while I'm getting back on my feet? I can skip out to my parents' house when you or she wants to visit."

"J-Fly. I'm a yes. And for my mom, she loves you. I imagine she won't have a problem with it. Let me check and see what she says."

"Sounds good, Trevor. I wasn't sure where to turn."

"You're like family. I'm glad you asked."

We hang up and less than two minutes later my phone is ringing.

"Trev?"

"She said, 'Of course!'"

"Oh, great. I really appreciate it."

And just like that, I go from sharing half a house with Ira to having a full house all to myself.

The house is big and empty. And secluded. I'm sitting by myself at the pond. Yes, the pond where Ira and Trevor first became friends.

I decide that I need to find a job. Not a lifelong career that I'm passionate about. But simply something to give me a steady paycheck and the ability to be able to rent something for myself.

Deloitte has a spin-off company called Resources Global Professionals, which still offers management consulting, but on a smaller scale. Instead of going into a client with a team of people, this company sends one or two consultants.

The draw for prospective clients is that they mostly hire folks who were previously at one of the "Big Four" consulting companies, yet charge them out at a lower rate.

What I like about it is the fact that someone can go in, do a project, and then take as long of a break as they want. Without getting paid during that break, of course.

But it's a good alternative for me. I'll be able to get a paycheck, health care, and the ability to be back in the workforce without a big commitment.

For my interview I'm hoping that the gap in my resume won't be a big deal.

"So, it looks like you took about a year off? What did you do?" the interviewer asks.

"I left Deloitte and took a backpacking trip around the world," I reply.

"Oh, wow, that sounds awesome. What was your favorite country?"

And for forty-five minutes we talk about how he always wanted to do something like that, which countries Ira and I visited, and what it's like to be on the road.

"So do you think you'd be a good fit for the job?" he asks.

"Yes, from my years at Deloitte and…." He cuts me off.

"Nah, it's all good. I know you'll be great at the role here. I just figured I should mark down something else we talked about other than travel," he says. "I imagine anyone lasting at Deloitte for ten years would do a great job here."

"Oh yes. I'm looking forward to getting back to work," I say, telling mostly the truth. I do want to work to make some money. I do want to regain my independence. I do want to be around other people. Being alone at the country house is starting to feel quite lonely.

"OK, great, we will give you a call."

On the drive home from the interview, I get a call from the person I interviewed with. "Joanne, you have the job. Can you start Monday?"

"Uh, yeah. Wow, that's a bit earlier than I planned--but yes, sure, why not," I say.

I have one weekend to find some decent clothes to wear for a full week at work.

I'm settling in to living without Ira. I'm mostly staying to myself. I've got a steady paycheck, a fun team of people I'm working with and a tough implementation that is keeping my mind away from what got me here. My project is in Parsippany, New Jersey just about twenty minutes from where I'm living.

Life is starting to make sense again. I'm slowly moving on and getting back my free-spirited nature. I'm starting to feel like my old self again. Competent. Determined. I'm not going to let a man hold me back

And then I get a call.

Ring.

Ring.

Ring.

I see from the caller ID that it's Ira calling

"Hello?"

"Hey Joanne, it's me Ira," he says.

I wait because he called me. I'm not letting him off the hook by starting the conversation.

"Can we talk?" he asks.

"Sounds like we are talking," I say a bit sarcastically.

"I mean in person," he says.

"Why would I want to do that?" I respond.

"I have some important things to say, and I think it will be better in person," he says.

"Anything you have to say to me, you can say over the phone," I say. I don't want to meet him to get all of my emotions mixed up again.

"I think I've made a mistake. I don't want to be broken up. I think we should get back together."

Silence.

"Are you there?" he asks.

"Yeah, I'm here. I'm just shocked."

"Shocked?"

"Yeah, shocked like in I finally got used to thinking about life without you and now you've changed your mind? Shocked as in I've uprooted my life, moved out of the living with you and now you've changed your mind?"

"I told you this would've been a better conversation in person," Ira says.

"There is no better way to have this conversation! My heart was shattered and now I'm finally picking up all the broken pieces and now you want to come back into my life?"

"Yeah, I'm sorry."

"I can't just forget these last few months. Of hoping and wanting you to change your mind. And it never happened. Now that I'm moving on is when you reappear?"

"Yeah, but...." he starts.

"Sorry, I can't hear any more. I have to go," I say.

"Will you think about it?"

"I'm hanging up," I say. And I do. My heart beats fast. It's a combination of being pissed off and confused. And pissed off again. How dare he try to come back into my life now? Where was he all those months that I tried to figure out what happened to us?

There's no way I'm letting him back in. My heart is too wounded.

And a week later, I get the same call. And a week after that. And weeks turned into months. He resorts to pleading. I resort to hanging up. Or not answering the phone. Then one day I answer the phone and he says, "I'm not going to call you back."

"What?"

"I think it's best for both of us to leave you alone. That if one day you are ready you will call me."

"Okay" I say. What I don't say is, "Don't hold your breath waiting for the call because it's not coming."

"J, I want to let you know that I love you, and I'm here for you," Ira says.

"Thanks for letting me know," I say before hanging up the phone.

Good, he's going to leave me alone. I can get back to my single life. I don't need him. My brain tells me all of this, but my heart says something different. I feel so confused.

I need to talk to someone. I call my friend Allison to let her know what's the latest. "Ira called to tell me he's not going to call anymore."

"What?" she says.

"Yeah, that is what I said. I don't think he needed to announce that. He could've just stopped calling, right?" I say.

"Yeah totally. What else did he say?"

"Basically, if I want him back, I can call him."

"Well, do you want him back?" she asks.

"You know how much he hurt me. He waits until I'm moved out of the house with him and moved on and then he asks me back. Where were all of these thoughts when I was still living there hoping he wanted me back?" I say.

"Well maybe he just figured it out," she says.

"Allison, I'm not looking for logic, I'm looking for a friend I can commiserate with."

"Oh well in that case, fuck him!" she says.

"Right. Fuck him."

We laugh.

"Some days, I do miss him though."

"Well, I'll go back to how I started this call, do you want him back?"

"Everything is so raw right now. I'm not sure I know what I want."

"I get it," she says.

"I'm glad I have you as a friend to talk through this. I wish we weren't 3,000 miles apart. We could talk through this over a Cosmo."

"Agreed. Love you," she says.

"Love you too."

And we hang up.

My heart is torn because some days I do miss him and can see us together. But most days I'm remembering how he dumped me. And how painful it all was. And I need to protect my heart. I need to close it off from love right now. I need to get back to focusing on myself.

Love is painful. Or really, losing love is painful.

Sex and the City (Without the Sex)

MAY 2006

AFTER STAYING AT THE COUNTRY HOUSE FOR A COUPLE OF months, I know deep down that it's time to go. I'm so appreciative of the generosity of Trevor and his mom, but they've hardly visited their house and I feel that it's because I'm here.

I've saved enough money for an apartment rental deposit and now have a steady paycheck hitting my bank every two weeks.

I respond to a Craigslist ad to share an apartment with two roommates in New York City's West Village. I'm living out a long-held dream of living in NYC and all the possibilities that it holds.

The apartment, the roommates, the 10011 Zip Code—it all seems like the perfect scenario for a great life.

Although I do wonder if there's something flawed with my character that no one would want to stay with me. Well, not "no one." Ira.

I leave the pond house and start living the "single in the city" lifestyle. It's a three-level apartment that I'm sharing with my two roommates: one single woman, Jen, and one single man, Akon. They are not a couple. He's definitely on the other team.

Their bedrooms are on the top level, the middle level has the kitchen and living area, and the bottom level is my personal space. The listing made it sound like it was on the ground level, but in reality, it is half ground and half under the ground, in other words, a basement.

But it doesn't matter.

I have the whole floor to myself and can see the ankles of people walking by while I'm in bed.

Beautiful Music

AFTER A FEW MONTHS LIVING IN THE CITY, IT'S LABOR DAY weekend and I don't have any plans or anywhere to be. Unlike the entire rest of New York, it seems. My roommates leave for the Hamptons.

Feeling like I'm the only person left in the city, I'm randomly walking around the desolate streets. I stop by Tower Records in SoHo. Notice a CD by Corrine Bailey Ray. Although I have never heard of her, something makes me buy it. I listen to her songs over and over in my apartment, and the music and lyrics seem like the most beautiful I've ever heard.

I'm watching the feet of couples passing by. The songs make me miss Ira.

I call.

Ring.

Ring.

Ring.

"Hey Ira." I hear lots of people in the background.

"Hey. You called."

"I did. What are you up to this weekend?"

"I'm at the Garden State Arts Center at a Sheryl Crow concert right now with Davie."

"Just the two of you?" I ask imagining that they may be on a double date.

"Yeah, just us."

"That sounds like fun. Although maybe a little gay," I say with a little laugh.

He starts laughing as well.

It's the first time we laughed together in months.

"I'm glad you called," he says.

"I was wondering if you had plans this weekend. If not, want to meet me in the city tomorrow?"

"No, no plans. I'd love to come over," he says.

"I'll text you my address. Enjoy the concert. Tell Davie I say hi."

"Great, see you tomorrow. I'm glad you called," Ira says.

"You said that already," I say with a smile.

"It's really true," he says.

"Great. See you then."

"See you."

The next morning, I get a phone call from Ira at ten.

"Hey, I'm in the city. Double checking your address."

I tell him my West 10th street and ask him where he is.

"Um, oh, just down the street."

"Cool. I'll see you in a little bit," I say.

"Right. See you then."

Ira arrives about ten minutes later.

We look into each other's eyes. It's like something out of a movie. All the hurt has fallen away. I hug him and he hugs me back.

"I've missed you," he says.

"I've missed you too," I say.

We stand in my front hallway and just look at each other.

"I thought you gave me a phony address," he says.

"What do you mean?" I ask.

"Well I went to the address that I thought you gave me, and it was the police station up the street," he says. "When I got there, I thought you were just fucking with me."

"Why would I do that?"

"I'm not sure. But I sure am happy to see you."

"I'm happy to see you too."

And then I kiss him.

And he kisses me back.

It all feels so right. My heart no longer feels broken. I'm no longer mad at him.

"Can we start over?"

"Yes, we can," Ira says.

Three days later, he is still here.

Once together we feel like we never stopped. We both realize that we couldn't live without each other.

Didn't want to.

Life shared is better than being apart

Three months later, he asks me to marry him.

New Jersey: Heart

2006

MY DAD'S HEART IS GETTING WEAKER BY THE DAY. HE needs an operation to make it stronger, but the doctors feel that his heart is not strong enough to survive an operation. We take it day by day. He's in good spirits yet he's hoping we can plan the wedding pretty quickly.

And so we do. We find a band, a photographer, and a florist all in record time. Ira and I go to The Liberty House in Jersey City, which has three things going for it: the view of Manhattan, a more modern feel than any place we've seen in New Jersey (meaning no chandeliers or gold carpeting), and the location—it sits right in Liberty State Park, where my dad used to take me when I was growing up. It was his favorite place to visit.

After we visit and confirm that it feels like "the place," I call my dad to get his opinion. "Book it!" he says after hearing the excitement in my voice.

Black Wedding

THE TIME HAD FINALLY ARRIVED. I, LIKE MOST GIRLS, HAD dreamed about my wedding day all my life. In my mind, I would walk down the aisle with my dad. But I was not wearing the dress that I'd helped design, made with fabric from my mother's wedding gown. That was still tucked away in a garment bag. Instead, I was wearing a black suit and was walking my dad down the aisle in a coffin.

April 29, 2007, was my wedding day. Or supposed to be. But on April 28 as my parents were driving to join us for the out-of-town guest reception, Dad did not feel well. He asked my mom to pull over into a rest area. There, she walked him to the closest table. He asked if she could get him a slice of pizza and a coke. When she came back, she saw him face down.

People came to help, and paramedics arrived quickly. They tried to keep him alive. Soon they were in the ambulance on the way to the hospital.

Ira, my soon-to-be husband, and I were just thirty miles away finishing up our rehearsal lunch with the bridal party. We were surrounded by our closest friends and enjoying the view of the Manhattan skyline. Ira's phone rang. It was my mom telling him my dad was in the hospital and was feeling weak. Ira grabbed the closest piece of paper he could find and wrote down the hospital information.

We rushed there in a state of shock.

"Please let him be okay," was all I could think.

I imagined that my dad, who was always joking, would say to us as we arrived, "I heard they had good Jello in this hospital and I wanted to try it." We would all laugh, and he would say he just was a little weak from all of the excitement. He would tell me not to worry and that he would be fine, ready to have our first dance at the wedding reception together. And then he'd ask again as he had that morning, "You didn't pick a really long song, did you?"

"No, Dad I picked a short and sweet one," I would assure him again.

Ira would joke around with him and say "Joe, you weren't trying to get out of that dance were you?"

But the reality was that we were still in the car and I was reading out the directions Ira had written down. As I flipped the paper over, I realized he had written on a page our minister had brought to the rehearsal. Typed on that paper were the words "Ira, do you take Joanne…." The dam broke that moment. Tears would not stop coming. My dad just had to be fine.

As we burst into the emergency room, we saw no smiling face. My mom sat on a plastic chair in a tiny room with her head in her hands crying. Why was she there alone and not with him? Then she looked at me and I knew. She said through her tears, "He… didn't…make… it." Ira and I hugged her, and we sobbed together.

This was to have been one of the happiest times of our lives. Now it was the worst. "His heart just stopped," my mom said. We sat there in total shock.

"You're still going to have the wedding," she said.

Without even thinking, or asking Ira, I said, "No. We will have the wedding one day, but it won't be tomorrow."

"But what about everyone who flew in from California, Spain and everywhere?"

"They will come back another time."

"What about the venue? The band? The…."

I looked at Ira to see if he agreed. "Babe, we'll do it another day," he said.

The doctor came and asked if we wanted to see my dad. Mom must have told him about the wedding because he asked if I was the bride. Each step we took towards his room I kept praying there was a mistake. Maybe he was still alive, and the doctor had him mixed up with someone else.

The sight of my dad on the metal table will live with me for the rest of my life. The thick plastic tube protruding from his mouth was the final blow. It seemed to be hurting him even though I knew that could not be.

That evening was a blur. The reality of what had to happen next was overwhelming. We needed to contact our venue, our photographer, videographer, florist, baker and every guest to tell them why we were postponing our wedding. At that time, forty of our out-of-town guests were just arriving for the expected party at the hotel.

I called my maid of honor, Allison, first. She had a book that I'd put together with all of the wedding information. "Don't worry sweetie," she said. "I'll call all of your vendors and let them know." She had been the maid-of-honor extraordinaire during the planning and would continue that role in the "unplanning."

"What about the party at the hotel? Will you cancel that?" I asked.

"What if I go there so when people arrive, I can let them know what happened?" she said. She was obviously thinking more clearly than I was.

Then we had to call 100 other guests—our aunts, uncles, cousins, and local friends. Ira made as many as he could but there were some I had to make on my own.

After the hours of calls, we went to the hotel to see our friends. Instead of getting hugs and kisses to wish us good luck on our lives together, we were embraced in a wave of emotion and love to give us support to somehow get through this.

My mobile phone rang. It was our florist. "I am so sorry about the news. What would you like to do with all of your flowers?" My flowers? I had not even thought about them. She had received the call the night before but everything was ready. All of the table arrangements, bouquets, and boutonnieres were just going to go to waste.

"Donate the rest," I said. "But I'd like the boutonnière for my dad to wear at the wake."

For days and weeks we were constantly reminded of the wedding-death connections. Instead of writing thank-you cards for the gifts we had received, we were writing thank-you cards for the flowers and Mass cards for my dad. Getting the mail became one of the most painful parts of each day. Card saying, "Congrats on the happiest day of your lives!" would arrive along with others, "Sorry to hear of your loss."

I wasn't sure how I was going to move forward. I couldn't help but wonder if this was the universe's way of saying don't get married. I knew that Ira was hurting as much as I was; he had been extremely close to my dad.

And eventually, he was the one I talked through all of my fun memories of Dad. We laughed together over my Dad's reaction to finding two open Total cereal boxes in Ira's cabinet. "I can understand having two boxes of Total Ira, but why two *open* boxes?"

Through all the pain, Ira was there for me, my rock. We had experienced so much together, from meeting on a red-eye flight from San Francisco to New Jersey. We spent eight years being casual friends via email, as we were always in other relationships. When we started dating, we were never apart more than four days, even though we lived on separate coasts. We left our corporate jobs and took an around-the-world backpacking trip together.

But now, going through this together and coming out stronger in the end made me realize he was the one I wanted to be with forever.

We rescheduled the wedding for a few months later. Working with our vendors, we were able to select a date that worked for all of them: July 8. I knew my dad would be there with us in spirit. I wish he could be there in person. When we talked about who would be the officiant at our wedding, we could think of no one better: Trevor.

Morristown, New Jersey: Pee on a Stick

MAY 2007

WHEN WE THOUGHT THAT WE WERE GETTING MARRIED IN April, people asked us when we planned on starting to try for a baby.

On the honeymoon, we said.

Since the doctors warned me that it could take a while to get pregnant due to some medical conditions, we weren't sure how long it would take. So, after the non-wedding date, after the funeral, after a couple of weeks of walking around in a haze we started trying.

"Whew. I feel like we just made a baby," I said to Ira one night.

"What do you mean?"

"That was different. I felt something shift when we were making love. I don't know how to explain it, but I think I'm pregnant."

"I've never heard of knowing right away, but if it's true, I'll be super happy."

"Yeah, me too. I have an appointment for my annual with my gynecologist next week. Let's see if they can do a pregnancy test and find out for sure."

"That's a great idea."

I'm at my gynecologist's office in the room with my nurse and a nurse in training who is about to take my vitals to get me prepped for the doctor.

"So, I think I'm pregnant," I say.

"Oh, wow, that is great news. When was your last period?"

"About three weeks ago."

"Three weeks ago?"

"Yes."

They give each other a look.

"Well, you can't know if you're pregnant without missing a period," the nurse says.

"Well, I just know. I can feel it."

"So let me get this straight. You feel pregnant? And you haven't missed a period yet?"

"Yes, that is what I am saying."

The nurses look at each other again and I can see a little eye roll happening.

"Can I take a test?" I say.

"You can't take a test until you've missed your period."

"So in another week."

"I'm going to be away in another week at a wedding in Napa Valley, California."

"Well, then, wait until you're back."

"I was hoping to know before the wedding, but that sounds impossible, so I'll make an appointment for when I come back."

"Yeah, science and all," she says with a smirk.

"Yes, science rules."

"Well, actually, you can do an at-home test. Just know that it's not as reliable as ours, but you can try it. And let us know how it goes. But make the appointment."

"Okay, I will," I say.

"The doctor will be in to see you in a few minutes."

They leave and start to shut the door behind them. But before the door closes I hear them bust out in a fit of laughter.

When my doctor comes in the first thing he says is, "So you think you're pregnant?"

"I do. I feel it and…."

He cuts me off. "I told you last year that it's going to take a long time for you to get pregnant. How long have you been trying?"

"A week."

"A week? A week? Talk to me after the test."

And that was the last time I mentioned being pregnant at that appointment.

When I left the examination room, I saw all the nurses looking at me.

"See you in a couple of weeks for that test," one said.

"Yes, see you then."

One of the nurses turned around abruptly, and I hear her stifling a laugh.

I got home and let Ira know that I couldn't take the pregnancy test.

"What did they say when you told them?"

"They think I'm crazy for feeling pregnant because it's just been a couple of weeks." I use air quotes when I say feeling.

"They said that?"

"Well, not really, but they laughed at me and exchanged some eye rolls. I guess it is to be expected since they saw my chart and all the things that I have stacked against me to get pregnant so quickly."

"I can't get tested by them until I've missed a period. "That's not a big deal. We will know in two weeks," he says.

"It's not a big deal, but I kinda wanted to drink at Lisa and Will's wedding since it's at a winery and all. And now I won't know whether to hold off or drink up," I say.

"I can also do an at-home test. The day I can test is the same as Lisa's wedding."

"Well, it will be a Napa Valley pregnancy test."

We fly to California and head to the hills—the hills of Napa Valley. We're staying at an Airbnb. I found one that was made in the traditional ryokan style—the same as where we stayed while we were on the island of Kagoshima, Japan.

The place is beautiful and peaceful, and it doesn't feel like we are in the United States.

"Are you ready to pee on a stick?" Ira asks.

"As ready as I'll ever be," I reply.

The morning that we're able to test. We take the EPT out of its packaging and read the instructions. "Seems easy enough."

We're in the bathroom, which is all concrete and tile and otherworldly. While we're waiting for the results, Ira asks, "What are you hoping to see?"

"Well, I really want to drink at the wedding," I say.

"Uh, what?"

"Just kidding, I hope that my feeling was right, and I really am pregnant."

"I hope so, too," Ira says.

"And really not only to show those nurses I was right," I say with a smile. "That will be a bonus though."

The minutes click by slowly. When it's time to check the stick, we look at each other and say we will look simultaneously. We countdown 3, 2, 1.

"Oh my God!" I say.

"Oh my God!" Ira says.

We hug and laugh and cry and laugh some more. "I guess this means you can't drink at the wedding," Ira says.

"That's okay," I say. "Oh boy, I can't wait to tell the nurses."

Epilogue: Current Day

2024

SEVENTEEN YEARS LATER, WE'RE STILL MARRIED. WE named our son Joseph after my dad.

And we've added Luke to our family. He's a terrier-mix rescue.

We've passed the travel bug down to Joseph. He's traveled to France, Italy, Sweden, Hawaii, Denmark, Japan, and closer-to-home places like San Francisco and Washington, D.C.

When people heard we were taking him to Europe, they tssked or came right out and asked, "What's there to do in Europe for a kid?"

Joseph loves wheeling his bag through train terminals, eating gelato while watching the waves crash down on a dock in Cinque Terre, Italy, eating *moules frites* in Annecy, France, cooking homemade pasta in Piacenza with the Italian cousins, and exploring the island of Gotland in Sweden.

All four of us share a conversation in the hammock while at our tiny cabin in Hudson Valley, New York. Joseph asks, "Dad, why didn't you just propose in the desert?"

Ira looks at Joseph, then looks at me. "Yeah, I think you're right," he says.

"Well then we wouldn't have this fantastic story," I say.

I look into Ira's eyes and we laugh.
I'm happy not moving.
For a bit.
The gentle motion of the hammock is movement enough.
Or is it?

Where Are They Now?

Trevor: Brooklyn, New York in his penthouse apartment with his wife Emily, son Eric, and their dog Roxy. He's the CEO of a startup. We continued our friendship over the years, creating new memories over incredible meals.

Peggy: Chelsea, New York and Phoenicia, New York, with her dog Ziggy. She's the reason why we have our cabin in Phoenicia down the road. Ziggy is best friends with our dog Luke.

Marius: Living in Florida, with his wife, Jolita, and daughters. They own two coffee shops and have the art from the photo shoot in Lithuania proudly displayed.

The Rocks: Made it safely to Marius's mother. She got to live out the last years of her life with the safety of her rocks near her. She was happy the rocks got out and had an adventure.

The slightly bigger than a dorm-sized refrigerator: It mostly lived in Ira's home office but spent some time in Ira and Joanne's bedroom until Joanne said, "Either that refrigerator goes or I go."

Acknowledgments

To my publisher Highlander Press, Deborah Kevin, and her team, Hanne Broter and Suzanne Tregenza, for making this book a reality.

To the places where I wrote: Phoenicia Diner, Urban Cowboy, Bettina, Woodnotes Grill, Seasons 52, and Maeve's.

For my friends who were always there for me during the process of writing this book: Megan Flinn, Nora Ring, Allison Estolas, Maribeth Rubenstein, Mark Delane, Jean and Jim Smith, Eddy Lopez, Jr, Stephanie Fritts, Camille Hart, Kathy Kane, June Shatken, Peggy Neu, and Trevor Sumner.

To all the folks we crashed with, stayed with, and met on the trip: The book would not be the same without you.

For my writing teachers, David Farley and Cliff Hopkinson, for teaching me how it's done.

To all the amazing women of The Women Who Write, LLC, who made me a better writer.

To all the writers of Gotham, who helped with early versions of the chapters.

To John Yearley, for helping me figure out the beginning, middle and the end.

To Don George, for helping me craft the story, and seeing my story as a travel writer.

To my amazing family for always being there for me.

To my son, Joseph Black, who always makes life more interesting.

To my husband, Ira L. Black, for sharing this adventure of life with me —and for always being my rock.

About the Author

Joanne Flynn Black took a break from her high-powered career in corporate America and embarked on a round-the-world backpacking trip. She has no regrets about this decision! In addition to publishing articles online, for newspapers, and magazines, her writing was included the travel book, *Italy from a Backpack*. She is a a board

Photo credit: Ira L. Black

member of The Women Who Write, LLC, and *In Motion* is her first full-length book. To learn more, visit https://launchb4.com/.

facebook.com/joanne.flynn.black

instagram.com/launchb4

tiktok.com/@joanneflynnblack

linkedin.com/in/joanneflynnblack

About the Publisher

Founded in 2019, Highlander Press is a vibrant, mid-sized publishing house dedicated to transforming the world through the power of words. We are deeply committed to diversity and bringing big ideas to the forefront. At Highlander Press, we help authors navigate the journey from initial concept through writing, editing, and publishing, culminating in the release of a book that not only fulfills a lifelong dream but also solidifies their expertise and boosts their confidence.

Our unique approach centers on forging strong, collaborative relationships with women-owned businesses across the publishing spectrum, including graphic design, marketing, launching, copyright management, and publicity. We believe in the power of community and operate by the mantra, "a rising tide lifts all boats." This philosophy not only enhances our business model but also ensures that our authors receive unparalleled support and opportunities to succeed.

Join us in making a mark in the literary world, where your voice is heard, and your message has the power to change lives. Visit us at highlanderpressbooks.com to start your publishing journey.

facebook.com/highlanderpress
instagram.com/highlanderpress
linkedin.com/highlanderpress
tiktok.com/@highlanderpress

www.ingramcontent.com/pod-product-compliance
Lightning Source LLC
Chambersburg PA
CBHW051617120626
46551CB00014B/1837